The Student's Guide to the Internet 2000–2001

Reviews of the previous editions

'From a UK student's point of view, this is by far the best book about the Internet'   *Internet Resources Newsletter*

'The *Student's guide to the Internet* sets out to describe every inch of cyberspace, and manages to do so in terrifying detail . . . It's worth buying . . .'   *The Guardian*

'This book . . . will bring you up to speed on what all the fuss over the Net is about. It sure tells you where to start when it comes to research and extraction of information . . .'
                    Free Radical student cyber magazine, *Glasgow University*

'I recommend it not only to students but to all those involved in education'   *New Academic*

'The authors have created an incredibly comprehensive and easy to use guide to using the Internet effectively'
                    Online and CD-ROM Review

'I would willingly recommend this book to all students and staff who need to find out more about the Internet and what it can do'
                    The Electronic Library

'. . . it has a direct approach and is perfect for beginners and inter-mediate student users alike . . .
I highly recommend this book to college and university students'
                    Managing Information

'A recommended book with the advantage of being excellent value for money!'   *Education Libraries Journal*

'Smart thing is to get yourself a copy of *The Student's Guide*'
                    Writing Magazine

The Student's Guide to the Internet 2000–2001

Ian Winship
Learning Resources Department,
University of Northumbria at Newcastle

Alison McNab
Pilkington Library, Loughborough University

Library Association Publishing
London

© Ian Winship and Alison McNab, 1996, 1998, 1999, 2000

Published by
Library Association Publishing
7 Ridgmount Street
London WC1E 7AE

Library Association Publishing is wholly owned by The Library Association.

Ian Winship and Alison McNab have asserted their right under the Copyright Designs and Patents Act 1988 to be identified as authors of this work.

Except as otherwise permitted under the Copyright Designs and Patents Act 1988 this publication may only be reproduced, stored or transmitted in any form or by any means, with the prior permission of the publisher, or, in the case of reprographic reproduction, in accordance with the terms of a licence issued by The Copyright Licensing Agency. Enquiries concerning reproduction outside those terms should be sent to Library Association Publishing, 7 Ridgmount Street, London WC1E 7AE.

First published 1996   Second edition 1998
Reprinted 1997   Revised second edition 1999
Reprinted, with amendments, 1997   This third edition 2000

British Library Cataloguing in Publication Data
A catalogue record for this book is available from the British Library

ISBN 1-85604-381-9

Typeset from authors' disk in Elegant Garamond and Geometric 415 by Library Association Publishing.
Printed and made in Great Britain by MPG Books Ltd, Bodmin, Cornwall.

Contents

Introduction to the Third Edition

From its first publication in 1996 we have always claimed there are three things that make this book different from the hundreds of other books about the Internet.

★ It is British.

Most books about the Internet originate in the USA, and although the Internet is international they still have a US bias in the information sources they cover. This one includes important UK sources you are unlikely to see in other books.

★ It is for students – and others in higher and further education.

We emphasize the Internet as an information and communication resource, and feature those sources most useful to support academic courses – including those available only to UK higher education. Because the book is short and concise it is affordable too! We don't specifically consider recreational and leisure information, but what you learn will be useful for finding that too.

★ It is realistic.

We don't claim that all you ever need to know is on the Internet, but we do show you what is important and how Internet resources complement other printed and electronic sources of information.

While it is no longer the only Internet book for UK students we believe it is still the best, being based on our many years of using the Internet with students and academic staff in all subjects.

Our aim remains simply to help you get the best out of the Internet for your studies. We try to accommodate all students, of whatever age, whether full-time or part-time, undergraduate or postgraduate, whether new to the Internet or not. We cannot tell you all you'll ever need to know, but we do show you the main procedures and sources to help you explore the Internet, build up your knowledge of how to use it, and find how it can be relevant to your particular needs. We cannot deal with all the local variations of accessing the Internet (whether at university/college or from home) so we do not discuss in any detail how to connect to it; nor can we do more than outline the principles of the many electronic mail systems in use or the main features of web browsers. You will need to find fuller practical details from your local computing service or library. What we do is to concentrate on the resources that are available to you.

While it would be useful for you to have a comprehensive guide to information sources for your own subject, to do so would need a book many times the size of this one, and much of the content would date rapidly, so we simply illustrate what is available and discuss major collections of subject information for you to consult as needed. In general we try to demonstrate principles and give examples, with suggested sources to go to for further information. Your own institution will have a web server providing local information and access to the Internet, which will give you an easy route to many of the sources we discuss.

Since the Internet changes all the time, and sources and websites come and go, we have tried to concentrate on the more established, stable and general sources that should be around for some time. In particular we have considered those intended specifically for UK education, financed or subsidized by the funding bodies for higher and further education to encourage the use of networked information. These are discussed mostly in Chapter 5 and are the sources you might find most relevant to begin with.

For this edition we have added some new sections on, for example, study skills and electronic journals; we have reviewed, checked, extended and updated the rest of the content, adding new resources where appropriate and removing those no longer available. Nevertheless, given the ever-changing nature of the Internet we cannot guarantee that all the addresses (URLs) given will still be valid when you try to use them.

Ian Winship
Alison McNab

1

What is the Internet and how can it help you?

★ Background
★ Access to the Internet
★ Statistics and demographics
★ What you will and won't find on the Internet
★ Academic use

During the 1990s the Internet caught the public imagination in a way few other technologies have done. Over this period access for the whole of society has moved from being restricted to a few sectors – higher education and larger companies – in the early 1990s, to an estimated 32.5% of the total population of the UK having online access by May 2000.[1] In the past year, advertisements for e-commerce sites have become common in all forms of the media and the growth of Internet-only companies – increasingly called *dot.com* companies – such as Amazon.com (worth $20bn in early 2000) represents one aspect of the e-commerce revolution.

So what is the Internet? Well, contrary to what some have said, it is not – yet – the greatest information source ever with the answers to all your questions. In essence, the Internet is an international network of computer networks – it links millions of computers around the world, and can be used for many different and ever-growing purposes. The Internet allows users to access different types of information (for example, documents and software) as if they were held on your own computer, and other people can read documents you choose to 'publish' on the Internet as if they were held on their own machine.

Students and staff in higher education are in a privileged position in having ready access to the Internet through JANET (the Joint Academic NETwork), which links higher and further education, and research centres in the UK. You will have access through your institution to one or more local area networks (the campus network), which provides links to JANET, and so to the Internet. The upgraded version of JANET, offering greater speed and capacity, is known as SuperJANET. The latest incarnation, SuperJANET4, is under development:

http://www.superjanet4.net/

This book discusses two main ways in which you can use the Internet: to communicate with other people, and to find information.

Communication can take the form of using electronic mail to correspond with a range of individuals or groups. This may be your tutor on campus, friends or family in other cities, or an 'expert' anywhere in the world. It can also consist of publishing your CV or a creative writing project (see Chapter 11), or finding factual information on the world wide web.

The sort of information which can be located on the Internet is extremely wide ranging. It ranges from data to assist in writing your final-year project (see Chapter 5) to adverts for jobs after you graduate (see Chapter 7). Chapters 8 and 9 describe complementary ways of searching for information.

Background

The Internet as we know it today developed from an experimental computer network in the USA in the early 1970s. Standard techniques enable different types of computer running different software to talk to one other and exchange data (information), so forming the seamless network that we know today as the Internet. The information that you send to other people (perhaps as an electronic mail message), or that someone requests from a host computer, is despatched by the software along what is perceived to be the most appropriate route, from network to network until it reaches the required destination.

Client/server technology underlies much of the Internet. Server computers disseminate information resources, and these are retrieved by client machines on global or local computer networks. In other words, you run a client program on your workstation which opens connections to remote computers, requests data from them, and receives and displays the resulting information. The server software runs on the remote computer you access, and can normally handle information requests from many clients simultaneously.

No single organization or individual controls the Internet, and for this reason it was often described as anarchic in the early 1990s. Nevertheless, there are key individuals and groups who monitor the Internet and who have influenced its development. The World Wide Web Consortium (W3C) was founded in October 1994 to realize the potential of the world wide web by 'developing common protocols that promote its evolution and ensure its interoperability'. Services provided by the Consortium include: reference information about the world wide web for developers and users; reference code implementations to embody and promote standards; and various prototype and sample applications to demonstrate use of new technology. Membership of W3C is open to any organization that signs a membership agreement. Its Internet address or URL (explained in Chapter 4) is:

> http://www.w3.org/Consortium/

The Internet Society (ISOC)
http://www.isoc.org/
is a non-governmental international organization for global cooperation and coordination for the Internet and its Internet-working technologies and applications.

The Internet Engineering Task Force (IETF)
http://www.ietf.org/
is the principal body engaged in the development of new Internet standard specifications.

The Internet Watch Foundation (IWF)
http://www.iwf.org.uk/
was launched in the UK in 1996 to address the problem of illegal material on the Internet, with particular reference to child pornography. It is an independent organization to implement the proposals jointly agreed by the government, the police, and the two major UK Internet Service Provider trade associations. Similar organizations have been set up in other countries.

The Internet was originally used by education and military researchers, but the recent huge growth in commercial use means that other organizations now exert a major influence. The widespread use of Internet products from computer and communications companies like Microsoft and Netscape (who market browsers – see Chapter 4) and Macromedia (which provides a range of tools for website development) sets standards that others have to meet to compete.

One source which provides valuable background information about the Internet and its applications is *LivingInternet.com* at
http://www.livinginternet.com/

Access to the Internet

During 2000, a major initiative will result in widespread Internet access for the further education sector. This will bring FE increasingly in line with higher education, where Internet access has been 'free at the point of use' (paid for by the Funding Councils). Students will therefore only incur costs (principally telecommunications costs) if they wish to dial in to the campus network from where they live or work. On many campuses an increasing number of halls of residence are being 'wired' to provide access for students with their own computer workstations, by direct connection or by dial-up.

Your institution will place some restrictions on your Internet usage. While some of these will be related to resourcing (eg you are likely to be allocated a finite amount of file storage space), others will relate to acceptable use and copyright. Chapter 3 discusses some aspects of netiquette or network etiquette, while Chapter 11 touches on the *JANET Acceptable Use Policy*. Your fellow students and your institution may suffer if you breach either the local or national guidelines on use of the Internet. Staff in your library or computing service should be able to advise you on local access conditions on campus, as well as providing guidelines on using the Internet effectively.

If you have your own computer workstation (with a modem or network card, and the appropriate software), you may be able to plug it into your campus network, which will have a link to JANET and thus to the Internet. Even if you don't have your own workstation, your institution will provide access to workstations, some of which may be available 24 hours a day.

There is an increasing concern about the 'accessibility' of the Internet for users with disabilities. A useful collection of resources for the visually impaired is available through *NetLearn*:

http://www.rgu.ac.uk/~sim/research/netlearn/visually.htm

Increasing numbers of students arrive at university or college with Internet access, while others will want to set up access from home or work; this may be particularly important for part-time students. Once you leave higher education you may likewise want continued Internet access. For off-campus access you will need to learn new techniques for minimizing the amount of time you spend online, and find a commercial Internet Service Provider (ISP) instead of using JANET. Since 1998, a growing number of ISPs have offered free access to the Internet, requiring only telecommunications costs to be found. During the early months of 2000, a number of companies announced free and low-tariff telephone call charges for Internet access. Selecting from the wide range of ISPs and telephone companies is therefore now a very complex choice.

For the latest comparative information about Internet Service Providers, it is advisable to consult the monthly magazines about the Internet that are published in the UK (see Chapter 13).

Listings of Internet Service Providers in the UK include:

The List
http://thelist.internet.com/countrycode/44.html

and

Internet Access Providers in UK & Ireland (InternetUK)
http://www.limitless.co.uk/inetuk/providers.html

Comparative information about the facilities offered by free ISPs is available from the *net4nowt* website
http://www.net4nowt.com/

and other listings of free ISPs include:
Free Internet Access in UK & Ireland (InternetUK)
http://www.limitless.co.uk/inetuk/free-access.html

and

Free ISP Index (Easy as 1-2-Free)
http://www.12free.co.uk/ispidx.htm

Individuals without access to the Internet through their place of work or study can access the Internet in cybercafés and a growing number of public libraries.

The EARL website provides a listing of UK *public libraries offering Internet access* (this can be browsed by town or local authority):
http://www.earl.org.uk/access/index.html

Listings of UK cybercafés are available from:
UK Index
http://www.ukindex.co.uk/cybercfe.html

and

Internet Magazine
http://www.internet-magazine.com/resource/cybercafes/
index.html

Alternatively, run a search on 'cyber cafe' in *Yahoo! UK and Ireland*
http://uk.yahoo.com/

Statistics and demographics

It is claimed that statistics can be made to prove anything and statistics concerning Internet size and usage are less precise than most, often relying mainly on estimates. Nevertheless, one valuable site for demographic and other Internet surveys is provided by NUA, an Internet consultancy and developer which specializes in projects for large organizations and software companies. Three of the main statistics and demographics sites are listed below:

NUA Internet Surveys
http://www.nua.ie/surveys/
includes business, social, technical and demographic surveys.

How Many Online?
http://www.nua.ie/surveys/how_many_online/index.html
provides an 'educated guess' as to how many people are online worldwide in a given month. In March 2000 this was 332.7 million.

CyberAtlas
http://www.cyberatlas.com/
also provides a selection of Internet demographics and statistics, particularly focusing on market size and usage patterns.

The relevant section of *Yahoo!* (see Chapter 8) includes links to a variety of services that provide these statistics:

**http://uk.dir.yahoo.com/Computers_and_Internet/Internet/
Statistics_and_Demographics/**

What you will and won't find on the Internet

This book discusses different information resources found on the Internet; the types of resources available include:

★ text: reports, articles, books, directories and databases
★ images: graphics, photographs and video clips
★ sound: speeches, music and real-time radio

★ software: freeware, shareware, evaluation copies and upgrades of
            commercial products
★ junk!

In general, information that costs a lot to collect and create, such as
marketing and other financial data, or that is primarily of commercial
value, is unlikely to be available free of charge on the Internet, except
where there are special arrangements for higher and further education (see Chapter 5). What you will find includes non-commercial
software, conference papers, background information on companies,
product information, trial or cut-down versions of software, the text
of out-of-copyright books, and web pages from a wide range of
providers including voluntary organizations, educational establish-
ments, local and central government and self-help groups.

While selling services and goods over the Internet has not proved
to be the money-spinner some companies had hoped it would be,
many organizations feel that they at least require an Internet presence and an increasing number of advertisements in all forms of the
media include URLs. Sometimes company sites can be disappoint-
ing, and may give little more information than a 30-second TV commercial. Others, particularly those from high-tech companies, will
provide valuable, useful data.

Where the Internet has proved to be invaluable is in relation to
information that will not be static for long enough to be published
in printed form (such as the lists of cybercafés mentioned on page
6) or that needs to be updated regularly (such as sports results).
Much information that is ephemeral and with little long-term value
is ideal for distributing via the Internet. Individuals with the time
and interest to collect information on their hobbies or leisure interests have found the Internet an ideal medium through which to
provide newsletters, fanzines, facts and figures, and even software.
However, enthusiasm and circumstances can change, so these types
of source can be short-lived. Topics that have a high profile in the
media and the professional press tend to be prominent on the
Internet as well. Thus you will find many web pages which deal

with GM foods, the environment, computers and the Internet itself.
The Internet is increasingly used for distributing resources found
in another medium – as a growing range of web versions of daily
newspapers and magazines demonstrates (see Chapter 6). Ultimately,
any information that you find on the Internet is only as good as the
provider makes it. It is important to be critical in relation to resources
that you find on the Internet, whether these are web pages, databases
or software. You need to consider whether these are accurate, comprehensive and up-to-date – the best web pages, for example, will
include information about the individual or organization that
authored them as well as the date on which they were last updated.
There is a difference between facts and opinions – learning to distin-
guish between these is important, but perhaps never more so than on
the Internet. Many companies will be seeking future employees who
have gained familiarity with the Internet and electronic communication while students, and the ability to think critically is one of the
most valuable benefits a graduate can bring to an organization.

Academic use

To trace books and journal articles for essays and assignments, you
will almost certainly have more success if you use your library catalogue or OPAC (online public access catalogue), and seek the advice
of library staff on the best indexing/abstracting services to use (see
Chapter 5). Alternatively, you may well use the Internet to access
your OPAC (or one at a nearby library) or an electronic database;
however, you will normally still have to go and fetch the book or
journal you want from the library shelves. More and more academic
journals are becoming available in electronic formats, though, and
the titles of those you have access to will probably be listed either on
the OPAC or your Library's web pages.

There is also a growing range of services which will offer to post,
fax or e-mail the full text of journal articles (including the *UnCover*
service, mentioned briefly in Chapter 6) but these should only be
used in emergencies as you will have to bear the cost yourself. Always

check whether your library subscribes to the journal in question and, if it does not, enquire about the interlibrary loan facilities available to you.

As early access to the Internet was most widespread amongst the academic and research community, it is not surprising that much information to be found on the Internet reflects this. Most universities and colleges now provide extensive information about their courses and research activities. In higher education, articles and books normally go through a process of evaluation by other experts in the field (this is known as peer review). How to replicate this process for Internet resources originating in the research community is still a matter of debate. There are some researchers who feel that the results of publicly funded academic work should remain in the public domain free of charge, and several pre-print archives (see Chapter 6) illustrate this. There is a real tension between those who see the Internet as a commercial opportunity and those who see it as a distribution medium for information, open to everyone in the same way a public library is, but on a global scale.

Although there is much talk of the 'electronic campus' or 'digital library', most academic institutions are still only beginning to explore the real possibilities and opportunities opened up by widespread access to the Internet. You will still read and generate much paper during your time as a student, but you can use networked resources to enhance the traditional sources of information to which you have access, to trace a lot of 'non-traditional' information, and to 'network' with people. The Internet makes the 'global village' more of a possibility than ever before, and during your time as a student you have the opportunity to explore and contribute to this – don't miss out!

Reference

1 *NUA How Many Online?* (July 2000)
   http://www.nua.ie/surveys/how_many_online/europe.html

2

Understanding and using Internet addresses

★ How Internet addresses are constructed
★ Why you need to know

Since the Internet comprises huge numbers of computers, and involves communication between them, there clearly needs to be a way of identifying each machine and this is done by means of an address.

Each computer on the Internet has a unique address (similar to a postal address or a phone number) to allow users to contact it, whether for e-mail, to call up information or use some software. The Internet Protocol, or IP, address is made up of four sets of digits, eg 223.332.33.5. This may sometimes be the same as the URL (Uniform Resource Locator) for a web page, but not always, as the URL (described in Chapter 4) can point to particular files on a machine. Your machine may have its own address but it is more likely you will connect to the Net through one – a university server or an Internet Service Provider if you connect from home – that does. Though computers use these addresses it is difficult for people to remember these numbers, so a variant system using names has become universal – you will rarely see an address in the numerical format.

These addresses are created in a database called the Domain Name System (DNS) and follow prescribed patterns.

All addresses have at least two parts – an organization name, and the domain (the type of organization), but may have three, four or five parts.

A typical address is that for the library catalogue at the University of Northumbria:

opac.unn.ac.uk

The parts of the address represent a particular **computer** – **opac** – at a particular **organization** – the University of Northumbria, here abbreviated to **unn** – in the **academic** domain – **ac** – and in a particular **country** – the UK. It is pronounced opac dot unn dot ac dot uk. Addresses are usually by convention printed in lower-case letters, though they could be written in upper case – it does not matter.

Other examples of academic addresses in the UK are:

ukoln.bath.ac.uk
a computer named UKOLN at the University of Bath
cs.staffs.ac.uk
the Computer Science department at Staffordshire University.

Non-academic organizations have other codes for their domain and often don't have a computer name, eg:

pavilion.co.uk
a company
nus.org.uk
a non-profit organization: the National Union of Students
coi.gov.uk
a government body: the Central Office of Information

Other countries' addresses have the internationally agreed country code and may not have a domain, eg:

info.funet.fi
Finland
www.springer.de
Germany

These can occasionally be used in other ways, such as the GCSE revision site *revise.it*, which uses the Italy code.

The exception to this format is the USA, which does have a 'us' code, but it is rarely used, as they have their own format without the 'us'. This is because they invented the Internet, just as British postage stamps have no country name because we invented them! Some international organizations are starting to use an **int** code. US addresses differ also in their 3-character domain names:

www.whitehouse.gov
government
microsoft.com
a company
comics.scs.unr.edu
an educational establishment
rs.internic.net
a network administrative body
nic.ddn.mil
a military organization
pubs.acs.org
a non-profit organization

However, many non US-based organizations now also use the **.com** domain, for example:

British Airways
www.british-airways.com/

or

the *Economist magazine:*
www.economist.com/

This is usually to give themselves a more international image or to reflect the international nature of their activities and is particularly seen as necessary for anyone involved in e-commerce.

We are also beginning to see variations such as **uk.com**. New domains, such as **.shop**, **.firm** and **.arts** have been proposed for some time, but have not yet been implemented.

Using addresses

You will need to use addresses when sending electronic mail (see Chapter 3) and when connecting to various remote resources using telnet or on the world wide web (see Chapter 4). However, for much of the time you may not need to key them in as your local web service will include the most popular ones, and you will build up your own collection of those you find most useful in a 'bookmark' or 'favorites' list (see page 37).

Nevertheless, it is always useful to know how addresses are put together. Sometimes you may spot a mistake in an address or you may not know the address of some particular organization you want to contact but can make a good guess what it might be. So a WWW (world wide web) machine usually has an address in the form *www.name.domain.country*, eg:

www.ox.ac.uk/

and commercial companies like to include an obvious version of their name, eg:

www.the-body-shop.com/

(though you might guess this one as www.bodyshop.co.uk or some other variant!).

Finding addresses

There is no overall list of Internet addresses to consult, but there are various ways of finding them.

If you need an address for electronic mail then some sources are discussed in Chapter 3. If you want to connect to a particular organization, and guessing the likely form of the address does not work, then you can try a subject collection like *Excite* or *Yahoo!* (discussed in Chapter 8) or one of the world wide web search services like *Google* or *Infoseek* (discussed in Chapter 9). The latter index millions of pages of information on the Internet, so will generally find those from any organization you specify and show the address. In some cases the search can be limited to words in the address only, and not in the text of pages, so simplifying the process.

3

Essential communication skills on the Net

★ Using electronic mail to communicate with individuals
★ Using discussion lists and newsgroups to share information and experience on a subject
★ Network etiquette – good practice in using mail

Electronic mail

The first use of the Internet for most people is to communicate with other users worldwide using electronic mail and as e-mail is becoming common you may already be a user. Nevertheless, please read on as familiarity with e-mail for personal use will not necessarily make you aware of features and uses for academic purposes.

E-mail is a means of sending a message – from a few lines to many pages – from your computer, or more likely from the space allocated to you on your departmental or institutional system, to someone else's space elsewhere. This person's space may be in your own institution or anywhere on the Internet. The process is generally quick – a few seconds to reach someone in your own institution; minutes, hours, or occasionally longer, to the other side of the world. (On a bad day it can take hours for short distances, especially if your mail system goes down, as can happen!).

You simply type in your message and the address to which it is to be sent, and send the message. The recipient has to check his/her 'mailbox' to see what messages have been received – it's a bit like a telephone answering machine. The most popular – if not strictly academic – use will be to keep in touch with your friends in other institutions free of charge, but your lecturers may well use it as an important means of communicating with you to distribute course information or assignment details. You may even be able or expected to submit assignments by e-mail or to have an online seminar. Other parts of your organization may use e-mail for administrative purposes; for instance, the Library, to remind you that books are due for return or to inform you that a requested book or article is now available.

To use e-mail you need to contact your computing service to get an account (no money is involved!) on your local computer system, which will have a mail facility. Conversely you may well be allocated an e-mail account when you register for your course. Even if you already have an account at home you should use your institutional e-mail as this address will normally appear in your institution's address book and so can be used by lecturers, library, administrative, computing and any other staff who need to contact you.

There are many different e-mail systems, such as Elm, Eudora, Microsoft Outlook, Pine, and Pegasus. Some use a Windows environment with menus to choose options from, others will require you to enter commands. Detailed procedures cannot be given here but your computing service will provide instructions.

All mail systems should allow you to:

★ edit a message offline before you send it
★ cut and paste text/addresses from and to messages
★ reply to messages received, quoting text from the original message if desired
★ forward a message you have received to someone else
★ store messages for future reference, if necessary in folders or directories
★ print messages
★ delete messages
★ create a mailing list to send a message to a group of people

★ send a file of text already created

★ save a message you have received as a file so that you can edit it

★ consult an address book of mail addresses at your university/college

★ set up an 'alias' – a short form of address – for frequently used addresses, so you can type 'jim' instead of 'james.simpson@ brighton.ac.uk'.

Figure 3.1 shows a typical message with a lot of information at the beginning (the header) relating to the route the message has taken. This may not always be present, or may be hidden by the software. Your address is normally added automatically to the header, but you should include your name (and, if appropriate, your university or college) and address at the end. Some people use a signature file like this one giving more information, or even a witty quote, which can be added automatically or easily to your message.

Mail messages are usually simple text files, though some can also create messages in HTML (the web-page language) or RTF (Rich

```
Delivered-To: tom.bradley@nowhere.ac.uk
Return-Path: <d,g,jones@somewhere.ac.uk>
X-Delivery-Time: 958727148
Received: (qmail 20382 invoked from network); 19 May 2000 09:05:48 -0000
Received: from heatwave.mail.pipex.net (158.43.128.224)
    by icestorm.mail.pipex.net with SMTP; 19 May 2000 09:05:48 -0000
Received: (qmail 17364 invoked from network); 19 May 2000 09:00:52 -0000
Received: from mailer2.smw.ac.uk (158.125.1.206)
    by depot.dial.pipex.com with SMTP; 19 May 2000 09:00:52 -0000
Message-Id: <3.0.5.32.20000519100045.00934400@staff-mailin.smw.ac.uk>
X-Sender: lisdgj@staff-mailin.smw.ac.uk
X-Mailer: QUALCOMM Windows Eudora Light Version 3.0.5 (32)
Date: Fri, 19 May 2000 10:00:45 +0100
To: "Tom Bradley" <tom.bradley@nowhere.ac.uk>
From: Danielle Jones <d.g.jones@somewhere.ac.uk>
Subject: Good book
In-Reply-To: <001101bfc111$bbaf5ce0$0908bc3e@oemcomputer>
Mime-Version: 1.0
Content-Type: text/plain; charset="us-ascii"


Tom

Have you seen the new edition of the Students Guide to the Internet? Well worth recommending to your students.

Regards

Danielle
=====================================================
Danielle Jones,  Department of Comparative Astrotheology,
Teac Building, University of Somewhere, Somewhere SM34 7TY

Tel 0224 1234 78              Email:  d,g.jones@smw.ac.uk
Home page: URL: http://www.smw.ac.uk/staff/~dgj
```

Fig. 3.1 *An e-mail message*

Text Format) to allow a variety of fonts or other ways of emphasizing text. However, since many mail systems cannot read these formats and would show the message as plain text there's no great advantage in using them. Most mail systems will also allow you to send more complex files, such as a word-processed document, a spreadsheet or an image, as an 'attachment' to your message. However, these can be very large files so, if you send an attachment, you need to be sure that your recipient's system can deal with it and that they have enough filespace for it. Many discussion lists (see below) discourage the use of attachments.

Some good practice

★ You should always put a useful title in the subject: line. Many people get lots of messages a day (perhaps 100 or more) and will scan their list of messages to see which to read first – and maybe delete uninteresting-looking ones without reading them.

★ The use of shorthand convention in messages is sometimes encouraged to save time, eg BTW – by the way; IMHO – in my humble opinion, but these should be used sparingly.

★ Similarly there can be the use of 'smileys' or 'emoticons' to add more meaning to messages, such as :-) for happy. There are large numbers of these, but their meaning is never very obvious and they are best ignored.

★ You need to manage your messages since you may have limited space for storing them. You should get into the habit of checking your message files regularly and deleting those you no longer need. It can be easy to acquire a few hundred messages, particularly if you are on discussion lists. It is often helpful to put saved messages into folders on different topics – it makes it easier to find them again!

★ Don't use long lines in a message as they will probably wrap round in other people's mail programs – around 70 characters is appropriate. Your mail program should allow you to set this length.

★ Plain text messages cannot include a pound sign so always spell out the word.

Free e-mail

As well as e-mail at your university or college, you will already have an alternative if you have Internet access at home or work, but it is also possible to have free web-based mail from general organizations like Excite, Hotmail and Yahoo! or specialist ones like the National Union of Students. There are dozens of such services and you can see a list at:

http://www.e-mailaddresses.com/

These have the advantage that you can use them from anywhere, rather than having to log on to a particular computer system. The reason they are free is because you probably have to endure advertising and the service may be poor, partly because all messages, even to someone in the same room, have to go via the web mail server, which for some services will be in the USA. They will not have the same facilities as a full e-mail service and because of the academic and administrative uses of e-mail noted above should not be used instead of your university system, since your university e-mail address is your 'official' one, not that from a web mail service. It may even be possible to use your university system from anywhere with a web browser and not just on-campus – you need to check with your computing service.

Viruses

You are probably aware of computer viruses that can, at worst, destroy all the work on your computer and, at best, just be a nuisance. People worry that these can be passed on by e-mail and you may see messages warning you not to read a message with a particular heading because it contains a deadly virus. Be reassured that an e-mail message CANNOT normally contain a virus. See:

Computer virus myths
http://www.kumite.com/myths/home.htm

Internet hoaxes
http://ciac.llnl.gov/ciac/CIACHoaxes.html
which give details of common hoax viruses.

However, if the message has an attachment, such as a word-processed document, then this could have a species known as a 'macro virus', though it is unlikely. Nevertheless you should make sure your university system, or your own PC, has anti-virus software that will warn you of viruses and allow you to deal with them. It is important to upgrade this software regularly. As a further precaution you should not open attachments or any files ending in **.exe** (known as executable files) from sources whose validity you are unsure of, though even this principle is not always helpful, as some of the latest macro viruses arrive in a message purporting to come from someone you know.

Spamming

Just as there is junk mail and junk faxes, so there is junk e-mail, or 'spam' as it is often known. Spammers acquire mailing lists and send their advertising to thousands of mail addresses. Messages may sometimes be for legitimate products, but mostly are inviting you to participate in some get rich quick scheme or to visit a particular adult website. Spam messages are often just a nuisance but they can slow down mail systems. Spam is usually obvious from the mail header and you can simply delete it without reading. If you want to prevent it reaching you then you can use filtering software that may be part of your mail system or that you can obtain, probably for nothing. This checks incoming mail for specified words and refuses any containing them. It can also be used for coping with your normal mail, but this sort of filtering is not especially effective and can exclude messages you want to see.

For more information see

Coalition Against Unsolicited Commercial E-mail
http://www.spam.abuse.net/

E-mail addresses

In Chapter 2 we showed how the address for a particular computer is formed. An e-mail address simply adds the identity of the person concerned in the form **person@place**. (Note that @ is pronounced 'at'.) This identity may be a string of characters like **vhf45**, which will usually be your ID to log on to your local system, or it may be a more meaningful real name. The place may be just the organization name or may be a particular machine.

Examples:
vhf45@gold.ac.uk
j.smith@leeds.ac.uk
mary.green@cs.wsu.edu

Finding addresses

E-mail addresses are allocated by the institution concerned so there are no comprehensive national directories as there are for telephone numbers. Finding someone's address may be tricky, but there are a number of places to try, although they may not always be helpful for students' addresses. You can search on first and last names, and possibly a place or organization too.

JANET Directory Service
telnet://directory.ja.net
login: dua
This covers many UK universities, but is cumbersome to use and inconsistent in what it finds – sometimes it won't find addresses that it has found previously.

UK University E-mail Addresses
http://www.rdg.ac.uk/InfOff/dir.htm
is a collection of links to many UK university e-mail directories.

Yahoo! People Search
http://ukie.people.yahoo.com/
You can use this directory to search for other people's addresses from countries throughout the world, and to add your own. You will need to register the first time you use the system. A guide to searching is available.

There are lots of other directories based on various published sources of addresses. They vary in their accuracy and may include out-of-date addresses. Many are concerned mainly with US addresses. Try:

Internet Address Finder
http://www.iaf.net/

Bigfoot
http://www.bigfoot.com/

Infospace.com
http://www.infospace.com/

MESA – Meta E-mail Search Agent
http://mesa.rrzn.uni-hannover.de/

Switchboard.com
http://www.switchboard.com/

Whowhere
http://www.whowhere.com/

Another website:
People and Organisations in the United Kingdom
http://http1.brunel.ac.uk:8080/x500/search-form-gb.html
allows you to search for addresses of individuals and organizations (mostly universities) in the UK. A similar form allows searches for people and organizations worldwide.

A directory specifically for student addresses (mainly US) is

StudentCenter E-mail Directory
http://www.studentcenter.org/e-mail.htm

The *Mailbase* service (discussed below) can be used to find the addresses of people who have subscribed to their discussion lists. These will mostly be in the UK:

Mailbase
http://www.mailbase.ac.uk/

If you know the institution someone belongs to – particularly a university – you may be able to find details on its web service. (See Chapter 4 for lists of web services.)

Discussion lists

A discussion list uses e-mail to create a worldwide forum to

★ discuss topics
★ ask and answer questions
★ pass on news
★ share information on a particular subject

and so on.

A similar function is provided by Usenet newsgroups (see below) with each list or newsgroup dealing with a particular topic area.

Lists tend to cover academic subjects more than newsgroups do, though there are also many for recreational topics. Subjects can be as varied as dance, databases, Derrida or disarmament.

A list will be based in one country – most are in the USA – but open for anyone anywhere to join, though the membership and content, may reflect that country. Some are intended particularly for students, such as

postgrad@mailbase.ac.uk
and
arch-student@lists.colorado.edu
for archaeologists.

You choose if you wish to join a list, and do so by sending an e-mail message to an address to register.

The message will be something like

```
subscribe econ-model Bill Brown
```

(if your name is Bill Brown). You do not need to include your e-mail address as that is extracted automatically.

You send this message to an address in the form:

```
listserv@thvm.cmu.edu
majordomo@thvm.cmu.edu
```

for most US-based lists, or

```
mailbase@mailbase.ac.uk
```

for those on *Mailbase*.

Registration is done automatically by a program and you will receive confirmation and instructions on how to use the list.

The *Mailbase* website noted above includes details of its procedures, and a user guide for lists using the Listserv program is at

http://www.lsoft.com/manuals/userindex.html

However, there is always a person – the list owner – whom you can contact if you have problems.

Messages are sent to the list address and normally distributed to all those who are registered on the list. (Note: the list address is in the form listname@somewhere – such as **lis-link@mailbase.ac.uk** – and is not the same as the administrative address shown above. Inevitably you will send something to the list instead of the administrative address, but don't worry – we've all made that mistake!). Some lists are 'moderated' and messages are processed by a person – usually to give some coordination, but occasionally to control what is being sent. There is no obligation to contribute to a list, and you will probably benefit just from 'listening in' to the discussion or reading news items.

Some hints on good practice in using lists can be found later in this chapter. You can also see some general background information at

Mary Houten-Kemp's Everything e-mail
http://everythinge-mail.net/

Finding what lists exist

There are tens of thousands of lists out there, and a number of directories exist to help you discover them. They will always include instructions on how to join a particular list. Be aware that lists do not exist for every subject you might want.

Academically oriented lists in Britain are mostly part of the Mailbase service. They have a central site

http://www.mailbase.ac.uk/

that lists all their lists and for each gives a description, a directory of all the members, and an archive of messages that have been sent to the list. You can search list names and descriptions by subject. If you find a list that looks relevant, you can check the message archive to see what sort of topics are discussed before deciding whether to join. (Figure 3.2 shows a section from a list of messages on the *psych-methods* list.)

Other directories have a worldwide coverage but do not include lists of members or message archives.

psych-methods archives - May 2000 (By Date)

Previous Month | Next Month | Other months | Search | **List Homepage**

11 **messages sorted by:** [author] [thread] [subject]

Starting: *6 May 2000 - 00:53 BST*
Ending: *18 May 2000 - 17:18 BST*

- CALL FOR PAPERS - FQS 2(1) *Katja Mruck (18 May 2000 - 17:17 BST)*
- ANOVA with (very) unequal sizes *Harcourt, Diana2 (15 May 2000 - 09:47 BST)*
- Re: Grouping aphasia and depression scores - visual guide *Thomas ZoégaRamsø (15 May 2000 - 08:24 BST)*
- Karnofsky *Anthoula Lioni (11 May 2000 - 19:27 BST)*
- Grouping aphasia and depression scores *Thomas ZoégaRamsø (11 May 2000 - 13:59 BST)*
- Re: Mauchlys test of Sphericity *Ruth Hatcher (10 May 2000 - 14:47 BST)*
- Re: Mauchlys test of Sphericity *Jeremy Miles (10 May 2000 - 14:20 BST)*
- Mauchlys test of Sphericity *Ruth Hatcher (9 May 2000 - 16:34 BST)*
- New QDA software demonstration and preview: free seminar *Ann Lewins (9 May 2000 - 11:45 BST)*
- Statistical Applications Short Courses *James S. Roberts (6 May 2000 - 00:48 BST)*
- Assessment Conference *James S. Roberts (4 May 2000 - 02:07 BST)*

Fig. 3.2   *Directory of messages in the archive of the Mailbase* psych-methods *discussion list*

Directory of Scholarly Electronic Conferences
http://www.n2h2.com/KOVACS
is produced regularly by a team led by Diane Kovacs at Kent State University and concentrates on scholarly lists worldwide. Only a brief description is included. You can search list names and descriptions or browse the lists for a subject area.

For a directory of all types of list, including the Usenet newsgroups described below, try

Liszt
http://www.liszt.com/
which has over 90,000 lists indexed, or

Tile.Net
http://tile.net/lists/

All these lists are usually for use by anyone wherever they are, but you may also find that your institution has lists for internal use only, perhaps general ones to do with computing support or related to particular courses. The latter is very likely if you are a distance learner.

Setting up your own list

You don't always have to rely on there being a discussion list on the topic you want since you can set up your own, say for an area of research, at Mailbase or one of the web-based services like *eGroups* (**http://www.egroups.co.uk/**). The process is straightforward. You then have to let people know of its existence so they will join. You might announce it on a related list or publicize in a newsletter that will reach your intended audience.

Usenet newsgroups

Usenet is one of the oldest uses of the Internet, being created in 1979 by students in North America who wished to link together people who shared common interests. Today it is a conferencing system in which any user can participate in the discussion of a wide range of topics covered by over 30,000 newsgroups. Each newsgroup contains articles or messages which may be grouped in 'threads' or themes. It has a similar function to discussion lists, and users can post (send) and reply to messages, mail interesting articles to themselves and usually access newsgroup archives. As with lists, some newsgroups are moderated, which means that articles are screened for approval before appearing in the newsgroup. The range of subjects is immense, ranging from very technical computing topics to the weird, the trivial and the downright obscene.

Usenet is in essence a huge continuously updated database that users must consult to read messages – they do not arrive in a mailbox. It requires a very large amount of storage space, so your university is likely to offer only a selection of newsgroups for access, probably limiting this to those which are primarily of academic interest. You can look at any of the newsgroups but will normally subscribe to (select) those you want to see regularly – only these will be displayed when you connect.

Newsgroup names are organized in hierarchies with a number of categories, including:

alt	'alternative' discussions
biz	business
bionet	biological sciences
comp	computer hardware and software, computer science
news	news about Usenet
rec	hobbies and leisure interests
sci	research in the sciences
soc	social issues and world cultures
uk	newsgroups specifically on UK topics.

Some examples are **alt.lefthanders, misc.health.therapy.occupational**, and **uk.media.tv.friends**.

To access newsgroups you will require software known as a

newsreader. In some cases this may be a text-based reader (such as Tin or Pine), but more likely a newsreading facility will be included in your web browser or e-mail system. Alternatively, if you are connecting from home you can download FreeAgent from

http://www.forteinc.com/getfa/getfa.htm

This is a useful offline newsreader, that is you download messages then disconnect and read them, so saving telephone costs.

Your computing service is likely to provide documentation on using Usenet and the newsreader(s) available locally.

Figure 3.3 shows a typical list of messages on the **alt.support. asthma** newsgroup using Microsoft Outlook Express. You can see the threads for 'Gastric Juices' and 'Cured of Asthma?'.

It is possible to spend (or waste!) a lot of time reading and contributing to newsgroups – while you may wish to keep up with newsgroups that are particularly relevant to your academic or spare time interests, do remember that there is life on the Net beyond Usenet!

Identifying newsgroups of potential interest can be done in a variety of ways – you can simply browse down the hierarchies accessible to you, or consult a listing such as *Tile.Net* (**http://tile.net/lists/**).

Not all institutions provide access to newsgroups, but you can

	Subject	From	Sent	Size
	Flovent or Serevent?	Chris	17/05/00 16:57	1KB
	animal model for asthma	gcouger	17/05/00 20:43	1KB
	Re: This it too weird	Sherry Bane	17/05/00 23:19	1KB
	Frustrated - 8 yr old and asthma	PeacfulRvr	17/05/00 23:47	2KB
	Great Diesel News!	Carol Nation	18/05/00 00:33	5KB
	Gastric Juices	Kandle	18/05/00 15:37	2KB
	Re: Gastric Juices	Chefchk	18/05/00 16:09	2KB
	Re: Gastric Juices	Steven D. Litvintchouk	18/05/00 23:59	2KB
	Re: Gastric Juices	Debi	19/05/00 00:28	1KB
	Re: Gastric Juices	JGause23	19/05/00 01:11	1KB
	Re: Gastric Juices	CBI	19/05/00 02:52	3KB
	Cured of Asthma?	JAYBIRD248	18/05/00 16:11	1KB
	Re: Cured of Asthma?	Randy Cameron	18/05/00 18:24	2KB
	Re: Cured of Asthma?	JAYBIRD248	18/05/00 21:17	1KB
	Re: Cured of Asthma?	Colin Campbell	19/05/00 03:49	1KB
	Re: Cured of Asthma?	Michael Hinsberg	19/05/00 10:57	3KB
	Re: Cured of Asthma?	JAYBIRD248	19/05/00 22:00	1KB
	Prevalance of Allergic Asthma	Robb C. Reed	18/05/00 16:47	1KB
	methylprednisolone	Rick Merrill	18/05/00 17:16	1KB
	Re: Just a venting	randall j crabtree	18/05/00 18:39	2KB
	Re: Your Doctor And Alternative Medicine	Brian Williams	18/05/00 20:32	1KB
	Re: Does Singulair work well alone?	JAYBIRD248	18/05/00 21:27	1KB

Fig. 3.3 *List of messages on the* alt.support.asthma *newsgroup using* Outlook Express

browse public Usenet services at *Deja.com*:

http://www.deja.com/usenet

or

RemarQ

http://www.remarq.com/

Each site that offers Usenet newsgroups will make its own decision about which newsgroups to offer and the size of newsgroup archives which it will make available. Because of the storage requirements some may keep only a week or two's messages, so you need to get into a regular routine of checking the newsgroups that interest you. It is possible to search the archives of the majority of newsgroups using services such as *Deja.com* or *AltaVista* (see Chapter 9). These searching tools make it possible to search for messages posted by particular individuals as well as for those on specific topics. You should therefore be cautious of the content of messages you post to newsgroups, as messages you post may be viewed by supervisors or potential employers.

Background information for new users of Usenet can be found in the **news.announce.newusers** newsgroup. This newsgroup normally includes regular postings of articles entitled 'What is Usenet?' and 'Frequently asked questions about Usenet'. The latter is an example of a FAQ or Frequently Asked Question. FAQs are introductory files of information on a topic reflecting the commonest questions people ask about it. Since newsgroups range in subject from the erudite to the exotic, FAQs can deal with topics such as the Blues Brothers, how to become an astronaut, and US government information on the web. Each FAQ is distributed on one or more relevant newsgroups and should be updated and reissued regularly. There are collections of them such as the

Internet FAQ Archives

http://faqs.org/

You can browse by category or newsgroup or search the whole collection.

Netiquette

Netiquette, or network etiquette, refers to the generally accepted standards of good practice in using e-mail, discussion lists and newsgroups. There is a need for some discipline to ensure that lists work effectively and that time and computer usage is not wasted. The following are some useful guidelines:

★ Remember that mail systems are not especially secure or necessarily private, so don't use e-mail for confidential or otherwise sensitive communication. Think of a mail message as being similar to a message written on a postcard. Remember also that messages can usually be traced back to the sender.

★ Lists and newsgroups are intended to be a civilized forum, and the bad temper, abuse or anger that might occur in a face-to-face discussion is not appreciated. (Such electronic anger is usually known as 'flaming'.) Remember that the law can be applied to electronic communication, so don't make comments about someone that could, for example, be libellous or racist.

★ Do not ask trivial questions on a list that could be answered more easily in other ways (eg by looking in a book). They are likely to be ignored.

★ Do not ask questions that would require someone to do your research or write your assignment for you. Ask specific questions, if necessary telling people what you already know, and don't expect long or comprehensive answers. A response is more likely from someone if it can draw on their experience.

★ Nevertheless, do not be inhibited by feeling ignorant or overawed by the presence of academic staff on lists – many others are beginners too. 'I'm new to this list so this may have been asked before' is often a useful introduction.

★ If you ask a question on a list it's good practice if appropriate to post a summary of the replies.

★ Be considerate to others and allow for their mistakes. Do not reprimand people for not understanding procedures properly.

★ Brief comments are more likely to be widely read and to generate replies.

★ Try to respond to queries if you have something to contribute – lack of response is disheartening.

★ Lists can be a useful place to distribute questionnaires, but keep them short and don't expect a huge response. Remember that a list membership will not be a properly constituted sample.

★ Do not send 'chain letters': they are an abuse of the system that can slow down mail for others.

If you want more extensive guidelines try
The Net: user guidelines and netiquette by Arlene Rinaldi
http://www.fau.edu/netiquette/net/

or

Netiquette
http://www.etiquette.net/

Other communication techniques

There are other communication techniques you may be involved with as part of your coursework, especially if you are studying as a distance learner.

Chat rooms are a familiar part of the Internet in general, allowing those logged on to have a dialogue by typing in comments and replies. These chat rooms are usually either general purpose or are related to recreational interests. In the academic context they will be set up for particular functions – a course, a module or maybe only a specific topic – and will be used to have an online seminar. There may be a tutor involved to structure the discussion.

Videoconferencing allows audio and visual contact between locations for purposes such as lecturing, demonstrations, meetings and seminars. If you are in a multi-site university you may find videoconferencing used between campuses. The equipment used is normally in a studio or lecture room and carried out over high quality lines but videoconferencing over the Internet is possible from PCs using a cheap camera. Your college is unlikely to use this technology, but you could do this if you have your own machine.

Earlier we discussed Usenet, and a similar technique to this, in that you have to connect to it to read information, is the bulletin board. You may find this used to distribute course management information such as assignments, course notes or changes to the timetable and may also allow some interactive discussion on course topics, again in a form of seminar. If your institution uses Microsoft Outlook for e-mail then the associated public folders may be used as a bulletin board.

4

Net techniques explained

★ URLs
★ World wide web
  Browsers
  Bookmarks and Favorites
  URL and bookmark managers
  Web servers around the world
  E-mail access to the web
  Mobile phones
  Caching and mirror sites
  Common problems
★ Telnet
★ File transfer protocol
  Finding FTP files
  Procedures
  Compression

Uniform Resource Locators (URLs)

The URL (or Uniform Resource Locator) is one form of Internet address, and is used to connect to servers, sites or pages around the world. URLs are a standard method of naming or specifying any kind of information on the Internet. The client computer that you use only needs to know what protocol (a set of data-exchange rules that computer systems use to talk to each other over the network) to expect of the desired information, and it retrieves it by that protocol.

The user or web author specifies the format and protocol by using an appropriate URL.

Note that URLs are case sensitive, so take care when copying them down. Web pages with a ~ (the tilde sign) in the URL are normally personal pages provided by an individual.

A URL will usually specify three things:

<method>://*<address>*/*<pathname>*

<method> is the general kind of protocol or method used to retrieve the document. This will be **http** for HTML documents on the WWW; **ftp** for FTP; **news** for Usenet newsgroups; and **telnet** for telnet sessions. The method **file** can be used to refer to local files.

<address> refers to the computer (server) where the information or documents are stored. HTML and FTP documents all have a server on a specific host computer. Telnet sessions have a specific destination computer. Newsgroups are the only exception – instead of a hostname, you provide a newsgroup (for example, **news:news. answers**). Newsgroups were described in the previous chapter, and telnet and FTP are explained later in this chapter.

<pathname> refers to the directory or file where the information is to be found. A URL for a directory usually ends with a / and that for a file with .htm or .html

Not all browsers require the **http://** prefix if the URL is for a website, and it is increasingly common for people to quote URLs without it as the majority of URLs that individuals deal with will be for websites. Browsers (see below) increasingly will 'fill in the blanks' if part of the Internet address is missing. For example, typing 'ibm' into the *Location* box in later versions of Netscape Navigator will take the user to the IBM website at www.ibm.com; typing a similar term into the Internet Explorer *Address* box will invoke the *msnSearch* facility which works in a similar way.

Here are some sample URLs and explanations:

http://www.nus.org.uk/nuscard.html
an HTML document – a document describing the NUS card.

ftp://rtfm.mit.edu/pub/usenet-by-group/news.answers/ftp-
   list/faq/
an FTP file (actually a FAQ) on a computer at the Massachusetts
Institute of Technology, in the sub-directory /pub/usenet-by-
group/news.answers/ftp-list/.

telnet://lib.dartmouth.edu
access to Dartmouth College Library Online System – the College
Library catalogue and other services.

World wide web

The world wide web (often abbreviated to WWW or simply the
web) is a hypertext-based system for finding and accessing Internet
resources; it is now the dominant way of using the Internet. It can
provide access to a variety of Internet resources from the same interface, including FTP sites and Usenet newsgroups in addition to
websites.

The world wide web is a distributed (in that it is not based in
any single location), multimedia (combining text, still and moving
images, and sound), and hypertext (containing links to other documents, allowing information to be retrieved in a nonsequential
way) system. It is thus a unique medium for communication and
for publishing.

In order to improve the speed of access to popular websites, a
mirror site (an exact copy) may be available in several continents.

Documents for the WWW are written in HTML (Hypertext
Markup Language) – see Chapter 11 for further information.

Browsers

To access the world wide web, you need browser software. Most UK
higher education institutions running Windows95, Windows98 or
Windows NT will run Microsoft's Internet Explorer. Other campuses or departments may run Netscape Communicator/Navigator

as the standard browser – partly because it is available for PC, Macintosh and Unix computers.

Your institution may also provide the Lynx browser. This is valuable for those who are visually impaired as it provides access to text information only, which can be read with speech-synthesizing software or enhanced screens.

Although the multimedia dimension is one of the main features of the web, if the information on the site you wish to consult is text-based you can choose to switch off the *images* (pictures or graphics) when surfing the web. This allows a browser like Netscape or Internet Explorer to operate in a similar way to Lynx. Unfortunately not all WWW sites are set up to allow viewing in text-only mode.

Browser features include the ability to:

★ copy (save) a file to disk – in text or HTML form
★ print a file; if it contains images the process will be slow, and you may need a colour printer for best results
★ search the text of the file currently displayed
★ cut and paste text to other applications within a Windows environment
★ open/go to a specific URL that you key or paste in
★ interrupt a slow or unsuccessful file transfer
★ mail files to yourself.

The requirement of seamless access to a wide variety of file formats (for example, PDF documents for electronic journals), Internet services (eg Usenet news) and audio and video files puts pressure on browser software. One solution is the development of modular browsers which allow additional plug-in or helper software to be added. Typical examples of the use of plug-ins are to access video or sound clips.

On campus, you are unlikely to have the opportunity to customize, upgrade or even choose the browser software that you have access to, but it can be helpful to be aware that solutions may exist, even if they cannot be readily implemented on your campus network. Similarly, not all multimedia features – such as audio or video files – may be available to you on public machines.

BrowserWatch
http://browserwatch.internet.com/
is a website with extensive information about browsers and plugins. It includes a list of browsers, and it indicates which computer systems each browser supports or plans to support.

See also the *CNET Topic Center on Browsers*
http://home.cnet.com/internet/0-3773.html
This includes links to tips and tutorials for both Internet Explorer and Netscape.

Some FAQs (frequently asked questions – and answers) on web browsers can be found at
http://www.boutell.com/openfaq/browsers/

Bookmarks and Favorites

A particularly important feature of browsers is the bookmark that records a document title and URL to enable you to revisit it when you wish to – just as a physical bookmark can take you to a particular page in a book. The bookmark feature on most browsers (called 'Favorites' in Internet Explorer) offers a short cut back to a specific document. This is particularly useful when you find a document purely by chance while browsing the Internet, as it might otherwise be difficult to rediscover the site. You will want to record sites that you visit regularly, such as your library's information pages. Bookmarks can be saved in order to pass them on to other people, or even used as the basis for creating a web page.

In Netscape, to bookmark the document that you are presently viewing you choose the **Bookmarks** menu option and then **Add Bookmark**. Next time you click on the Bookmarks menu, the bookmark should appear in the list. To revisit that site in future, all you need to do is click on the name of the document in the bookmark list. Similar facilities are offered within Internet Explorer, except you choose the **Favorites** menu option and click on **Add to Favorites**.

Both Favorites and Bookmarks can be rearranged into groups of nested folders, which permits you to create a personal catalogue of useful Internet resources organized in a way that suits you. If you invest time developing and organizing your bookmarks, do back them up regularly.

You can also put bookmark *shortcut* icons on your desktop – these will allow you to launch a web browser, connect to the WWW and access the desired site in one go. In both Microsoft Explorer and Netscape go to your chosen page, right-click on the mouse and choose **Create shortcut**. A shortcut icon will be created, and you simply double-click on this.

Further information on organizing and using Bookmarks and Favorites can be found through the Help options for both Netscape and Internet Explorer. A number of tutorials are available including:

> http://netforbeginners.about.com/internet/netforbeginners/
> library/weekly/aa110799.htm

A simple alternative to bookmarking sites (which is particularly useful if you are not using your own workstation at the time) is to mail the text of documents to yourself or to other people. In Netscape this can be done by using the **Send Page** command on the **File** menu; you may need to set up details of your e-mail address before you can mail a message (select **Preferences** from the **Edit** menu, then the **Mail & Newsgroups** menu and then select **Identity**). Using Internet Explorer, select **Mail & News** from the **Tools** menu, then choose **Send a Link**. If the subsequent message you receive includes a hot-linked URL, then your e-mail software is probably set up to take you directly to that site.

URL and bookmark managers

If you travel, move between machines, or keep losing bookmarks because you forget to back them up, one solution may be to use one of the growing number of URL and bookmark managers. These sites host your bookmarks/favorites on a web page with password access, after you have registered. Existing bookmarks/favorites can also be imported.

Free bookmark managers include:

BookmarkBox
http://www.bookmarkbox.com/

BookmarksPlus
http://www.bookmarksplus.com/

Clickmarks
http://www.clickmarks.com/

ItList
http://www.itlist.com/

Murl
http://murl.com/

MyPassword.net
http://www.mypassword.net/

Other services are listed at:
http://www.davecentral.com/urlman.html

Web servers around the world

The number of websites is vast and growing rapidly and it is impossible to list them all. None of the attempts to do so are complete, and you may need to use the search services described in Chapters 8 and 9 to trace the sites you want. However, collections or directories of web servers in particular subject areas or geographical regions can be of value.

Company sites

Company A-Z (UK Yell)
http://www.yell.co.uk/ukyw/atoz/index.html
An alphabetical listing of commercial and business sites in the UK

UK Index
http://www.ukindex.co.uk/index.html

Government

Open.gov.uk is the entry point for UK public sector information, at
http://www.open.gov.uk/

Higher and further education

Universities Worldwide covers 147 countries and over 5000 institutions:
http://geowww.uibk.ac.at/univ/

An alternative source is *BRAINTRACK,* covering 152 countries:
http://www.braintrack.com/index.htm

Within the UK, the University of Wolverhampton *UK sensitive maps* of web servers covers

★ universities and HE colleges
http://www.scit.wlv.ac.uk/ukinfo/uk.map.html
★ FE and other colleges
http://www.scit.wlv.ac.uk/ukinfo/uk.map.colls.html
★ research sites
http://www.scit.wlv.ac.uk/ukinfo/uk.map.res.html

Libraries

UK Public Libraries on the Web (Sheila and Robert Harden)
http://dspace.dial.pipex.com/town/square/ac940/weblibs.html

Schools

UK Schools on the Internet
http://schools.sys.uea.ac.uk/schools/schools.html

The voluntary sector

CharityNet aims to provide an international guide to non-profit data, links, sites and resources available on the web:
http://www.charitynet.org/

Charity Choice also provides an encyclopaedia of UK charities on the Internet:
http://www.charitychoice.co.uk/

E-mail access to the web

Occasionally you may only have limited access to the Internet because of hardware limitations. However, it is possible to access almost any Internet resource using e-mail. Simple e-mail commands can be used to access FTP, Usenet and the world wide web. Even if you do have full Internet access, using e-mail services can save you time and money. However, try to limit your data transfers to one megabyte per day, and don't swamp the servers with many requests at a time.

To retrieve web documents by e-mail, all you require is the URL which defines the address of the document. You can retrieve the text of that page by sending the e-mail message send URL (substituting the URL for the site you wish to access for URL) to an Agora web-mail server (there are several located around the world).

To obtain a document (*Accessing The Internet By Email – Guide to Offline Internet Access*) listing these servers and with full instructions on how to retrieve WWW pages (and other services) by e-mail, send an e-mail message to:
mailbase@mailbase.ac.uk

In the body of your message, enter only this line:
```
send lis-iis e-access-inet.txt
```

Mobile phones

Just coming into use as we write are mobile phones that can connect to the Net using Wireless Application Protocol (WAP). These have a small screen and can display web pages that have been written or adapted especially for this purpose. Thus the content is limited and the pages are simple compared with most web pages these days. Information is orientated to consumers – events, news headlines, sports results, train times – and as yet there is little academic information available in this way.

Caching and mirror sites

The difficulty posed for networking staff who have to support a high demand for Internet access is considerable. Anyone who has tried to access a website in North America at 4pm knows how slow the response time can be! While some of the reasons for this are discussed below (see Common problems), one technique which helps to improve both the response time for web end-users, and also reduces the network loading, is caching. The idea is to enable a local server to keep copies of the web pages that have recently been browsed. The next time someone else wishes to access those resources, the browser can retrieve its pages from the cache rather than returning to the remote server and re-fetching pages which someone else at your site or in your neighbourhood already has on their hard disk. In addition to easing network congestion, this can save on bandwidth costs. UK higher education institutions use the National JANET web Caching Service, at
   http://wwwcache.ja.net/
Occasionally caching can create a problem if the pages you are looking for are updated several times a day (for example news or sports results) and the copy in the cache does not reflect this.

However, it is possible to retrieve the most recent copy of a document by clicking on the 'Reload' button on your browser.

Many organizations block access from the Internet to their network(s). This prevents people outside the organization from gaining access to sensitive information – this procedure is known as a *firewall*. Where organizations have a firewall in place, it may be necessary to go through a *proxy server* before connecting to the Internet. Proxy settings and caches can affect access to electronic journals and databases; your IT support staff should be able to advise.

Mirror sites are an alternative means of conserving bandwidth and speeding up retrieval. A mirror service is an exact copy of a complete website, software or files held in another geographical location. Publishers of electronic journals may have mirror sites for the Americas, Europe and Asia, for example. UKOLN offers mirrors of several library and information science journals at:

> http://mirrored.ukoln.ac.uk/lis-journals/

Common problems

Some problems you may encounter when using a browser to access the web include the following messages:

Error 404 – 'Not found' – is possibly the most common error message. It means that the document you requested cannot be found on the server. The URL may have been typed in wrongly, or the web pages moved to another server or removed from the web altogether. Alternatively, the web server you are trying to reach may be temporarily inaccessible – it is always worth trying later or the following day.

Error 400 is a 'bad request', which means that something is wrong with the URL you typed. It may be that the server you're contacting doesn't recognize the document you're asking for or you may not be authorized to access it.

Server timed out: sometimes error messages are caused when the server you are trying to reach is too busy. This can result in the above message. If this is the case, you should try again at a less busy time (normally mornings and weekends).

Connection refused by host: this means that you may not be allowed to access the document or site. This is normally because it is password-protected or restricted to access from a particular domain. This is similar to *Error 403* – 'Forbidden'.

Failed DNS lookup: means that the DNS or domain name system (which maintains a database for converting between domain names and IP addresses) cannot connect from the URL to a valid Internet address. This can be the result of of a mistyped URL (specifically, a mistyped host name) or a harmless 'blip'. This can often be resolved by using the Reload button. If there is still a problem, it can be worth trying to connect an hour or so later.

There are several explanations if pages take a long time to load. Your local network or one of the networks used to connect to the required site may be busy (often described as a bandwidth problem), or the remote server may not be able to cope with the number of 'hits' it is receiving. It is always worth using the option in your browser to turn off graphics (images) to speed up the load time, or trying to reconnect at a different time, preferably in the morning in the UK.

HTML coding can get garbled or links in a page may have been mistyped – which will mean the intended page is not retrieved. In such cases it can be worth trying to modify the URL. This might involve substituting lower for upper case, a hyphen for an underscore character or vice versa. To see if the site is live, try going up one level (deleting the last part of the URL to the nearest slash), then check to see if there is a link to the document you are looking for.

The problem of accessibility has been touched on in Chapter 1 and in the discussion on browsers. If you use older browser software, you may find that you are unable to access some websites because they use Java. Java is a computer programming language that can be used to create complex applications on the web (animations, simulations, and multimedia). Further information on Java can be found at

http://www.sun.com/java/ or http://www.javaworld.com/

Further information on connection difficulties and error messages is available at:

http://www.livinginternet.com/w/wt.htm

Telnet

Telnet is the basic Internet command used to make a simple connection to a computer somewhere. Typically this computer will have some sort of large searchable database, such as a library catalogue, a collection of references on a subject or statistical information. Many sources that used telnet access are now on the web so that the use of telnet has become rarer.

The command is in the form

```
telnet address
```

For example, you type

```
telnet bcmsv.leeds.ac.uk
```

for an English verse collection at Leeds University.

With Windows or on a Mac you may have an icon for telnet on which you double-click and then enter the address in a dialog box. Alternatively, with a web browser enter the URL

telnet://bcmsv.leeds.ac.uk

If you are using a command line interface such as with a Unix or VMS system, the telnet command is made from the system prompt, such as a $ or %.

Occasionally you will also have to enter a username or password, but you will normally be shown on the screen what this is. (It will be the same for everyone.)

You may also be asked for a terminal type, perhaps choosing

from a list. Unless you know otherwise reply VT100. (The terminal type affects the screen layout, so if the layout is not right – for example, if it contains garbled characters – then you have the wrong terminal type.)

If you have telnet software on your machine (a telnet client in the jargon) then it will open in a window with drop-down menus for commands. You may need little other than the File/Exit command for when you are not disconnected automatically from the service you are using. Some software has commands from the keyboards. The most likely ones are

CONTROL–B to send a break or interrupt command to the remote system if you need to stop some process, perhaps because you have made a mistake
CONTROL–Q to quit from telnet.

You can see a list of the commands by keying help at the **telnet>** prompt.

Telnet merely makes a connection to a computer – it has no search capability – and you will find that the databases you connect to with telnet may all be different in the way they work. You will probably need some instructions on how to use them, but these should be available online.

There is no complete directory of addresses of 'telnet-able' resources, but a useful route to many, including bulletin boards, library catalogues and databases, is Hytelnet at
http://www.lights.com/hytelnet/
This gives you lists from which you can connect to the service you want. To find other services using telnet, check the subject guides discussed in Chapter 8.

File transfer protocol

File transfer protocol, usually abbreviated to FTP, and sometimes known as anonymous FTP, was one of the first uses of the Internet to transfer files between computers. Though other techniques can be used, FTP is still important. It is used much less for text than it once was, because of the ease with which the web deals with text, but it remains a much faster way of transferring software, data collections and images between machines. Typically it can be ten times faster, which can be significant if you are using a slow dial-up connection from home.

Until fairly recently the only way to use FTP was with a separate FTP program, but now a graphical web browser does the job more simply. It will sometimes use FTP without you knowing, for example if you download something such as software to your machine, but at other times you will need to go through a little more lengthy process.

Finding FTP files

You will come across references to FTP files in printed publications and on the Net itself. Usually you will know where to get them but if you have only the name of the file you will need to find a location. Lists include:

Lycos
http://ftpsearch.lycos.com/

Monster FTP sites list
http://hoohoo.ncsa.uiuc.edu/ftp/

Registry of FTP mirror sites on JANET
http://www.ftpregistry.mcc.ac.uk/
which lists overseas sites that are mirrored (copied) in the UK.

If the file is a program, you can try a software archive like *UK Mirror Service* or *SunSITE* (see Chapter 6); otherwise use the *Archie* service.

Archie

Archie provides access to an index of millions of files stored in over 1500 archives across the world. You can search it for a particular filename, or in a very rudimentary way by subject for specific words that might appear in the name or sometimes in a description.

With a web browser use *ArchiePlex* at

http://archie.emnet.co.uk/forms.html

You then simply fill in a box with the filename, and a list is returned with live links to the archive sites so that you can retrieve the file immediately by clicking, if you don't want to page through the whole list.

Procedures

We will assume you are looking for an update to the McAfee Virus Scan software called update4076.zip which you know can be found at the URL

ftp://ftp.mcafee.com/pub/antivirus/datfiles/update/update4076 .zip

(Files are held in a hierarchy of directories – 'pub' means public.)

With a browser like Netscape or a Windows FTP program like WS_FTP or RapidFiler getting files is simple.

In Netscape or Explorer you merely edit the Go To box or use the Open button and key the URL to get directly to the file you want. (Normally Netscape will automate the logon procedure, but occasionally you may need to enter the username 'anonymous' and your e-mail address as the password.) You will then be able to save it, usually to wherever you want. However, there may be associated readme or help files or you may want to browse up and down directories to see what else is available so it may be better to omit the file name so as to connect to the directory containing the file. Here the list of files is displayed, showing the name, filesize, date created, etc. You then select any required.

With FTP software you can put in the full file path (the URL above without the filename) or you may have to navigate the hierarchy of files to the directory and then select the file to save.

Older versions of FTP software, such as those using the MS-DOS operating system that predated Windows, require a more cumbersome procedure needing commands to be keyed in to list directories or choose files to be retrieved. You are unlikely to need this.

Compression

Many files available by FTP are in a compressed form – that is, they have been processed to reduce their size so as to reduce storage needs and speed up transfer. They then have to be uncompressed after transfer. Filenames ending in *.zip* (as in our example), or *.z*, *.tar* or *.zoo* indicate compressed files.

Normally if your browser has the appropriate helper applications configured you should be able to decompress the files once they have been retrieved by clicking on **Extract**. However, you may need to run a decompression program like *PKZIP* or *WinZip*. Such programs may exist on your local system.

If in any doubt about what to do, contact your computing service.

5

Subscription and JANET web databases

★ Features and use of electronic databases
★ JANET services
★ Passwords and off-campus access
★ Major collections of databases
   BIDS
   EDINA
   MIMAS
   Arts and Humanities Data Service
   NISS
   OCLC FirstSearch
   Cambridge Scientific Abstracts
★ Other databases

Other chapters in this book deal with information resources that are freely available to any users of the Internet. This one differs in that the resources discussed are available only on subscription to universities and colleges, usually arranged via your library – but don't be concerned, these charges are not passed on to you. More-over, the range of these electronic databases available to you will include only a selection of those listed. Obviously the larger univer-sities or colleges, which teach a wide range of subjects, will offer a greater range of sources. Your library is likely to provide web pages or handouts listing what is available.

Features and use of electronic databases

Electronic databases, such as those described here, together with the CD-ROM and other web-based services that may be available in your library, can be used to identify articles and other publications in particular subjects as well as numerical or statistical data. You may need to consult library staff to decide which of these sources is most appropriate for a specific purpose – a printed index may still be best in some subjects!

Many of these services are known as *bibliographic databases* – they will provide references to journal articles but do not include the full text, although some databases can link directly to the full text of the journals to which your library subscribes. Once you have identified and selected relevant references, you will then have to check whether your library subscribes to the journals which contain the full text of the articles. In some cases the electronic database can link directly to the library catalogue to do this. Many bibliographic databases also provide abstracts – a brief summary of what the article is about.

Most electronic databases originated as printed publications, and your library will probably hold earlier years in printed format. The electronic ones may be sufficient for many subjects where only recent material is needed, but for others like chemistry or history the printed indexes for earlier years are still important. You will find that electronic databases can be searched more quickly and allow you to combine search terms in ways which are not possible with printed services.

Databases can normally be searched for articles of interest using:

★ title words or phrases
★ authors
★ keywords
★ words in the abstract
★ institutional affiliations

or other identifying information.

After you have located references, you can display them on the terminal. You may be given an option to mark references which you want to follow up. These can then be printed, sent to your e-mail account, cut-and-pasted into another Windows application, or downloaded into a database. Your institution may provide guidelines on how to cite references, or see *Cite them right!* (discussed in Chapter 12).

In addition to bibliographic databases, many libraries are providing increased access to full-text information in electronic form. Applications in this area include: electronic journals, British standards, engineering product data, company information, market reports, newspaper reports, online encyclopaedias in art, and structured online textbooks. These can be searched and browsed and, in most cases, data or excerpts can be included in your assignments.

JANET services

There are a number of electronic databases and datasets accessible over JANET which are funded or subsidized by the *JISC: the Joint Information Systems Committee* – see

http://www.jisc.ac.uk/

Some of these have been available to the higher education community for a number of years, but most are now also offered to further education institutions. They mostly are made available from a small number of providers as collections of databases in various subjects and are described below.

Some of the databases and texts available from *MIMAS* and the *Arts and Humanities Data Service* may be used as raw data in your studies, in conjunction with appropriate software. For example, you may analyse electronic versions of texts by Chaucer obtained from the *Oxford Text Archive*, or use Census data to discover more about the different types of housing in your area. Company or financial information from commercial providers may be downloaded into spreadsheet software and manipulated in a variety of ways.

Passwords and off-campus access

The majority of these services require a username and password, which may be issued automatically, obtained from your library or computing services, or provided online. For many of the services discussed in this chapter the username/password will be issued by the *ATHENS* service. The *ATHENS* authentication system **http://www.athens.ac.uk/** provides controlled access to many major services with a single ID. Others, however, will have their own usernames and passwords.

Accessing the electronic services discussed above may present particular difficulties if you wish to access them from off-campus. Certain electronic products check the Internet address you are logging in from and may restrict access only from your own campus; these are restrictions placed by the information provider. Your library and computing services staff will be able to advise you on your local situation. *ATHENS*-authenticated services can be accessed both on- and off-campus.

You will then be able to use these services free of charge in connection with your studies as the subscription will have been paid by your university or college, or directly by JISC. The conditions of use are displayed when you access each database, but the majority may be used for academic purposes only. Where this is the case, commercial use is forbidden – for example, using these services to gather information for your employer if you are a part-time student or on an industrial placement.

You should be able to use these services from any terminal in your institution that has JANET access; your library or computing staff will be able to advise you on accessing them from halls of residence or off-campus. Searching these databases, and following up the information retrieved, may be your most productive use of the Internet in relation to your studies.

Major collections of databases

Services hosted by BIDS

BIDS (Bath Information and Data Services)
http://www.bids.ac.uk/
is an electronic data service which hosts a range of bibliographic databases, as well as linkages to its *ingentaJournals* full-text delivery service, allowing users to access electronic journals if their institution holds a subscription. All *BIDS*-hosted databases include extensive online help screens, and references may be printed, sent by e-mail or downloaded. *BIDS*-hosted services include:

★ *BIDS BLII*: a large, multidisciplinary bibliographic database based on 20,000 of the most requested titles from the British Library Document Supply Centre (BLDSC).

★ *BIDS CAB HEALTH*: covers all aspects of human health and disease (emphasis on disease epidemiology, prevention, diagnosis and treatment, immunology and pathology). Comprehensive coverage of HIV and AIDS.

★ *BIDS Education*: provides access to two major bibliographic databases for education: *ERIC* and the *British Education Index (BEI)*. The *BEI* covers 350 British and selected European English-language journals, as well as national report and conference literature. *ERIC* indexes over 775 journals.

★ *BIDS EMBASE (Excerpta Medica Database)*: a major pharmacological and biomedical literature database covering 3500 journals from 110 countries.

★ *BIDS IBSS (the International Bibliography of the Social Sciences)*: a database covering 2400 social sciences journals world-wide and around 7000 books per annum. Coverage goes back to 1951. This extensive database covers economics, sociology, politics and anthropology.

★ *BIDS ISI*: The BIDS ISI service was withdrawn in July 2000. The ISI datasets are now hosted by MIMAS and known as *ISI Web of Science* (see page 58).

★ *BIDS PASCAL*: international coverage of literature in science, technology and medicine.

★ *BIDS Reuters Business Briefing Select*: full-text news articles from over 1000 English language sources around the world.

★ *ingentaJournals*: full-text access to thousands of academic and professional journals (see Chapter 6).

★ *INSPEC*: provides access to the international scientific and technical literature in physics, electrical engineering, electronics, communications, control engineering, computers, and computing and IT.

★ *MEDLINE*: covers all areas of medicine, including clinical medicine, experimental medicine, dentistry, nursing, nutrition, psychiatry, and health service administration.

★ *RAPRA*: provides references to articles, conference papers and technical publications on processing, properties, testing and application of polymers, plastics, rubber, adhesives and composites.

★ *RSC*: a range of databases supplied by the Royal Society of Chemistry, including *Analytical Abstracts*, *Chemical Business NewsBase*, *Chemical Safety NewsBase* and *Mass Spectrometry Bulletin*.

For further information, help or advice on searching any of the *BIDS*-hosted services, consult their web pages or ask your library staff. User guides are available for most *BIDS*-hosted services:
http://www.bids.ac.uk/info/serviceguides.htm

Services hosted by EDINA

EDINA (Edinburgh Data and Information Access)
http://edina.ed.ac.uk/
based at the Edinburgh University Data Library, provides national online services for the UK academic community. Services include databases in agriculture, environment and life sciences; arts, humanities and social sciences; and engineering, informatics and physical sciences. References may be e-mailed, and a number of the

services include links to full-text electronic journals in cases where your library holds a subscription. Services include:

★ *AGDEX*: an extensive database of over 85,000 article titles or abstracts from the agricultural press, compiled since 1971 by the Scottish Agricultural College (SAC).

★ *Agricultural Census*: Agricultural Census data (includes over 150 items of information on agricultural activity in UK farms) spanning the last 25 years.

★ *Art Abstracts and Art Index Retrospective*: bibliographic coverage of 280 leading art periodicals – journals, museum bulletins and yearbooks. *Art Abstracts* covers from 1984, with abstracts after 1994. *Art Index Retrospective* covers leading international art journals published between 1929 and 1984.

★ *BIOSIS Previews*: the electronic format of *Biological Abstracts* and *Biological Abstracts/RRM*. Comprehensive coverage of international life science journal and meeting literature.

★ *CAB Abstracts*: covers research and development literature in the fields of agriculture, forestry, aspects of human health, human nutrition, animal health and the management and conservation of natural resources.

★ *Digimap*: Digimap allows users to view and print maps of any location in Great Britain at a series of predefined scales. Maps may also be downloaded for advanced cartographic tasks.

★ *EconLit*: indexes and abstracts more than 550 international economic journals.

★ *Ei Compendex*Plus/Page One*: *Ei Compendex*Plus* is a comprehensive interdisciplinary engineering information database covering journal articles and conference proceedings. *Ei Page One* provides tables of contents to engineering journals.

★ *Environmental Sciences & Pollution Management Databases*: multi-disciplinary database covers all areas of air, land, water, and noise pollution.

★ *INSPEC*: provides access to the international scientific and technical literature in physics, electrical engineering, electronics, communications, control engineering, computers and computing and IT.

★ *MLA International Bibliography*: Covers literature, modern language, folklore, and linguistics from a number of different countries and cultures.

★ *PAIS International*: a bibliographic index with abstracts covering the full range of political, social, and public policy issues.

★ *SALSER*: an online information service about serials held in Scottish academic and research libraries, including all the university libraries, the National Library of Scotland, and major city libraries.

★ *UKBORDERS*: the online service for extraction of digitized boundary data for the UK. The data can be used for computer-aided mapping of the small area statistics from the 1991 Population Census.

★ *Ulrich's International Periodicals Directory*: a unique, current, comprehensive and continuously updated source of information on selected periodicals and serials published throughout the world.

Copies of *EDINA* quick reference cards may be available in your library; they can also be downloaded from:
    http://edina.ed.ac.uk/docs/doclist.html

Services hosted by MIMAS

MIMAS (Manchester InforMation and Associated Services)
http://www.mimas.ac.uk/
is a national dataservice based at the University of Manchester. It specializes in online provision of research and teaching datasets, software packages, training and large-scale computing resources for the UK academic community.

Services available through *MIMAS* include the 1991 Census of Population Statistics, government and other large continuous surveys, macro-economic time series data banks, digital map datasets, spatial geo-referencing datasets, full-text electronic journals and scientific datasets. Specialist support is available, including training courses, comprehensive documentation, software support and statistical advice relating to the datasets and the associated data access/analysis software. There is access to software packages and the large-scale computing resources required for data storage, access, manipulation, and analysis/visualization. These computational facilities are also available to users wishing to analyse their own large and complex datasets which require either large amounts of disk space/CPU and/or access to specialist software not available locally.

MIMAS services include:

ISI Web of Science
http://wos.mimas.ac.uk/

There are three citation indexes (*Science Citation Index*, *Social Science Citation Index* and *Arts & Humanities Citation Index*) containing details of articles drawn from about 7500 international journals from 1981. [Your lecturers may have used this service when it was previously hosted by *BIDS*.] There is a facility for cited author searching – that is, looking for recent papers that have referred back to a known relevant paper. Also included is the *Index to Scientific & Technical Proceedings* (*ISTP*) containing details of papers presented at over 4000 conferences per year. An extensive range of user guides is provided at:

http://wos.mimas.ac.uk/documentation.html

JSTOR:
http://www.mimas.ac.uk/jstor/
JSTOR is a unique digital archive collection of core scholarly journals starting with the very first issues (many of which date from the 1880s) and made available to subscribing UK higher education institutions. Over 110 journals in a variety of fields are accessible.

ESRC/JISC Census Dissemination Unit
http://www.census.ac.uk/cdu/

MIMAS – Government & Other Continuous Surveys
http://www.mimas.ac.uk/surveys/

MIMAS – Macro-Economic Time Series Databanks
http://www.mimas.ac.uk/macro_econ/

MIMAS Spatial Data Help and Information Web site
http://www.mimas.ac.uk/maps/

MIMAS – Scientific Datasets comprises:

Beilstein CrossFire Chemical Information System
http://www.mimas.ac.uk/crossfire/

Cambridge Structural Database
http://www.mimas.ac.uk/scientific/csd/csd.html

and the

Mossbauer Effect Reference Database
http://www.mimas.ac.uk/scientific/merd/merd.html

Certain *MIMAS* services may require you to register before using them in addition to using *ATHENS* (exceptions are *ISI Web of Science* and *JSTOR*). Registration forms for most *MIMAS* services can be obtained from your local computing service or via the *MIMAS* website. In order to be able to access a particular dataset, it may be necessary to complete a separate individual registration form to become an authorized user. Information and advice about site and user registration procedures for *MIMAS* and/or particular datasets may be found at
http://www.mimas.ac.uk/regn.html

Services hosted by the Arts and Humanities Data Service

The *Arts and Humanities Data Service* (*AHDS*)
http://ahds.ac.uk/

is a national service funded by the Joint Information Systems Committee (JISC) to collect, describe, and preserve the electronic resources that result from research and teaching in the humanities.

The *AHDS* is a distributed service, comprising a number of service providers:

Archaeology Data Service
http://ads.ahds.ac.uk/

The History Data Service
http://hds.essex.ac.uk/

The Oxford Text Archive
http://ota.ahds.ac.uk/

The Performing Arts Data Service
http://pads.ahds.ac.uk/

The Visual Arts Data Service
http://vads.ahds.ac.uk/

Through the above services, the *AHDS* aims to facilitate collaboration amongst providers of networked information, services, and systems, whether commercial or not-for-profit, in the UK or abroad, in order to promote scholarly use of electronic information in the arts and humanities.

The *AHDS* has a substantial collection of electronic texts, databases, images, and mixed media resources of relevance to humanities disciplines. It also provides information about similar resources which are located and managed elsewhere.

Services hosted by NISS

Services hosted by *NISS*,
   http://www.niss.ac.uk/
include:

The *NISS Biomedical* service
http://biomed.niss.ac.uk/
which comprises a range of bibliographic and full-text biomedical services. These include the *Medline*, *CINAHL* and *Cancerlit* databases. Full-text access to a range of major medical and nursing journals is provided.

The *NISS Business & Industry Service*
http://www.niss.ac.uk/b+i/
provided by Responsive Database Services Inc, comprises the *Business & Industry* database providing extensive coverage of business and industry news. New records are added daily.

NISS Clover Service
http://clover.niss.ac.uk/
lists indexes to newspaper and magazine articles.

NISS Computergram Service
http://www.niss.ac.uk/news/computergram.html
is a daily newspaper for the computer industry, covering company news, financial results and analysis and share dealing, plus news about developments and new products.

Services hosted by OCLC FirstSearch

OCLC FirstSearch
http://www.uk.oclc.org/oclc/menu/home1.htm
is an electronic reference service for end-users, consisting of a collection of electronic bibliographic and full-text databases covering books, journal articles, theses, computer software and other types of material. Around one-third of UK university libraries subscribe to a selection of *FirstSearch* databases. The databases available include popular commercial databases such as *ERIC* and *Medline*, as well as databases unique to OCLC:

WorldCat: an online union catalogue to many libraries around the world. It contains more than 40 million records (for books, computer data files and programs, maps, manuscripts, musical scores and videotapes) describing items on thousands of subjects published since about 1000 AD.

ArticleFirst: contains details of articles published in nearly 12,500 journals in science, technology, medicine, social science, business, the humanities and popular culture. Coverage is from January 1990.

ContentsFirst: contains the complete contents pages from individual issues of journals in *ArticleFirst*.

OCLC FirstSearch can be accessed via the web at
http://newfirstsearch.oclc.org/
A guided tour of *FirstSearch* is available at:
http://www.oclc.org/oclc/fsbi/frame_tour_newfs.htm

Services hosted by the Cambridge Scientific Abstracts Internet Database Service

The *Cambridge Scientific Abstracts (CSA) Internet Database Service*
http://www.csa1.co.uk/
provides access to a collection of more than 30 databases in fields such as the biological sciences, aquatic sciences, engineering and technology, environmental sciences, materials science, computer science and social sciences. Extensive user help is available, and search results may be sent by e-mail. Features of the service include the opportunity for libraries to provide links to their OPAC and/or full-text electronic journals from within the databases.

Databases available include: *Aluminium Industry Abstracts, Aids and Cancer Research Abstracts, ASFA: Aquatic Sciences and Fisheries Abstracts, Biological Sciences, Biology Digest, Biotechnology and Bioengineering Abstracts, Ceramic Abstracts/World Ceramics Abstracts, Computer and Information Systems Abstracts, Conference Papers Index, Copper Data Center Database, Corrosion Abstracts, Electronics and*

Communications Abstracts, Engineered Materials Abstracts, Environmental Routenet, Environmental Sciences and Pollution Management, ERIC, Findex, Internet & Personal Computing Abstracts, Linguistics and Language Behaviour Abstracts, Materials Business File, Mechanical Engineering Abstracts, MEDLINE, METADEX (Metals Abstracts), Microbiology Abstracts, Oceanic Abstracts, Plant Science, Safety Science and Risk Abstracts, Social Services Abstracts, Sociological Abstracts, Solid State and Superconductivity Abstracts, TOXLINE, Water Resources Abstracts and *Water Resources Routenet*.

Examples of other databases

ABES (Annotated Bibliography for English Studies)
http://abes.swets.nl/abes/
provides references to journal literature and books in the fields of language, culture, literature and film. Includes material from Africa, Asia, Australia and Canada.

AMADEUS
http://amadeus.bvdep.com/
a financial database of the top 200,000 public and private companies in Europe.

Applied Science and Technology Abstracts
http://hwwilsonweb.com/
indexes trade and industrial publications, journals from professional and technical societies, and specialized subject periodicals in all engineering and applied science subjects.

ASSIAnet
http://www.assianet.co.uk/
is an index to international English language journals covering the applied social sciences.

BHInet
http://www.bhinet.co.uk/

is a wide-ranging index to arts, politics, society and the humanities in British journals and magazines.

British Nursing Index
http://www.optonet.net/
covers major British and other English language publications relevant to nurses, midwives, health visitors and community staff.

Caredata
http://www.nisw.org.uk/lins/cd.html
provides abstracts of journals, books, government reports, research papers, and publications from the voluntary sector relevant to social work and social care.

ESDU
http://www.niss.ac.uk/cgi-bin/esdu.pl
is an online library of engineering design data. Access to over 1200 validated design guides, organized into subject areas in structural, mechanical, aeronautical and chemical process engineering. Reports on technical data for engineering.

FAME
http://fame.bvdep.com/
is a financial database of major public and private British companies. Includes company addresses, balance sheet figures and lists of products.

International Civil Engineering Abstracts
http://www.anbar.com/cgi-bin/ce/CEdb
which indexes and abstracts more than 150 civil engineering and building science journals.

Literature Online
http://lion.chadwyck.co.uk/
provides the full text of more than 2000 works of English and American poetry, drama and prose.

Mintel Marketing Intelligence
http://www.mintel.com/
provides online access to Mintel's market research reports. Institutions have the option to subscribe to all or some of the following
series: finance, retail, market, leisure, industrial.

6

Help and information for your course work

★ Subject sources – full text, research papers, bibliographies, images, numerical data
★ Specialist sources – electronic journals, software, newspapers, reference, government
★ Library catalogues
★ Teaching and learning material

Though there are a huge number of information sources on the Internet of many types – databases, research reports, numerical and statistical data, images, the text of books and journal articles, newspapers and so on – they still provide only a fraction of the information to be found in the printed books and journals and CD-ROMs that you will have in your library. Nevertheless, Internet sources are growing in importance because of their easy availability, immediacy and multimedia nature.

This chapter gives some guidance as to the sorts of information available, with examples, and directs you to more comprehensive lists online where they exist.

An important source that will be mentioned in various contexts is *NISS: Information for Education*

http://www.niss.ac.uk/

– a government-funded information service for higher and further education. It has material on the working of education – policy documents and so on from government departments and agencies, higher education information services, school performance tables, courses and conference information. It also gathers together much information for day-to-day use, such as:

★ addresses of universities and other institutions
★ research databases and other sources
★ job vacancies
★ reference sources such as dictionaries, e-mail directories, yellow pages, maps
★ financial information
★ electronic newspapers and magazines
★ library catalogues
★ software
★ collections of Internet resources arranged by subject
★ even TV and radio schedules.

It can often be a useful first place to look and will also be mentioned in other sections of the book.

Types of subject source information

Information sources dealing with specific subjects – such as a bibliography or image of a painting – are vast in number and to list even a representative selection of these for all subjects would be beyond the scope of this book. Here we merely explain what sorts of information you *might* find for your subject and give some examples of these.

Text of books

These are sources giving the complete text of out-of-copyright books. They can be viewed online or downloaded to a local file. Some of the material, especially in the humanities, will also be available in printed form (though it may not be easily accessible to you), but the electronic version is useful if you want to do any sort of analysis or merely to quote some text in your own work.

You will not normally find student textbooks on the Internet, since publishers still wish to make a living by selling books rather than by offering free information electronically, though there are some pilot projects looking at making recommended texts available in this way.

These are some general collections:

Oxford Text Archive
http://ota.ahds.ac.uk/

Internet Public Library Online Texts
http://www.ipl.org/reading/books/index.html

Project Gutenberg
http://www.promo.net/pg/

Online Books
http://www.cs.cmu.edu/books.html

Centre for Electronic Texts in the Humanities
http://scc01.rutgers.edu/ceth/

Specialist collections (which may include journal articles) include:

British Poetry 1780–1910: a hypertext archive
http://etext.lib.virginia.edu/britpo.html

Education-line
http://www.leeds.ac.uk/educol

Making of America
http://www.umdl.umich.edu/moa/

There are primary sources from the 19th century in many subjects, for instance:

Marx/Engels Archive
http://csf.colorado.edu/psn/marx/

Victorian (British) Women Writers Project
http://www.indiana.edu/~letrs/vwwp

Historical Text Archive
http://www.msstate.edu/Archives/History/
Provides worldwide historical material.

Research papers

Accounts of research have normally been published in a journal or conference paper, but increasingly researchers are publishing on the Internet to shorten the time needed to make their work available to other users, as well as to widen that availability.

Cogprints: Cognitive Science Eprint Archive
http://cogprints.soton.ac.uk/

Los Alamos E-print Archive
http://xxx.lanl.gov
http://xxx.soton.ac.uk
An archive for new research papers in high-energy physics.

Economics Working Papers Archive
http://econwpa.wustl.edu/Welcome.html
Collects papers from around the world on economic topics for retrieval and discussion.

NetEc
http://netec.mcc.ac.uk/NetEc.html
Bibliography of printed research papers; collection of electronic working papers.

PrePRINT Network
http://www.osti.gov/preprints
Preprints in energy and related disciplines.

PubMed Central
http://www.pubmedcentral.nih.gov/
Primary research reports in the life sciences.

Bibliographies and databases

Web databases, like those from *BIDS* and *FirstSearch*, that are available to higher education on corporate subscription have been described in Chapter 5, but there are also others which are accessible to anyone free of charge. They are likely to cover a fairly limited area, and you will not find them for all subjects. Their coverage of sources may not be as systematic as those available in your library, which will be needed for more comprehensive searching.

Anthropological Index Online
http://lucy.ukc.ac.uk/cgi-bin/uncgi/Search_AI/search_bib_ai/ anthind
indexes more than 750 anthropological journals.

Collection of Computer Science Bibliographies
http://src.doc.ic.ac.uk/computing/bibliographies/Karlsruhe/ index.html

Hytelnet
http://www.lights.com/hytelnet/ful/ful000.html
lists sources available by telnet, and gives access to databases on topics as diverse as Beethoven, astronomy and archaeology.

Internet Movie Database
http://uk.imdb.com/

Medline
http://www.healthworks.co.uk/
http://www.ncbi.nlm.nih.gov/PubMed/
Medline as a subscription database is mentioned in Chapter 5. These free versions may not have as many features or be as reliable.

PubSCIENCE
http://pubsci.osti.gov/
Covers physical sciences.

RAM (Recent Advances in Manufacturing)
http://www.eevl.ac.uk/ram/

Research Index
http://www.researchindex.co.uk/
is an index to business and industry news in UK newspapers and
trade magazines.

Science Policy Information News
http://wisdom.wellcome.ac.uk/wisdom/spinhome.html

Social Science Research Network
http://www.SSRN.com/
is a US collection of databases relating to economics, accounting
and financial economics.

Other databases will be included in the subject directories listed in
Chapter 8 and the search tool collections in Chapter 9.

Subject dictionaries and encyclopaedias

Dictionaries and encyclopaedias on the Internet may merely be versions of those in printed form or may be especially created by taking
advantage of the ease of collaboration allowed by the Net.

The most general one is the long-established

Encyclopedia Britannica
http://www.britannica.com/
which in its printed version used to be very expensive, but is now
available free on the web.

Subject ones include:

Academic Press Dictionary of Science and Technology
http://www.harcourt.com/dictionary
A dictionary also available in print or on CD-ROM.

Dictionary of Cell and Molecular Biology
http://www.mblab.gla.ac.uk/~julian/Dict.html

Encyclopedia of Law and Economics
http://allserv.rug.ac.be/~gdegeest/

International Financial Encyclopedia
http://www.euro.net/innovation/Finance_Base/Fin_encyc.html

Free Online Dictionary of Computing
http://wombat.doc.ic.ac.uk/

Encyclopedia Mythica
http://www.pantheon.org/mythica/

Stanford Encyclopedia of Philosophy
http://plato.stanford.edu/contents.html

Listings of online dictionaries, including foreign-language ones, can be found at:

Glossaries and Dictionaries
http://www.encyberpedia.com/glossary.htm

A Web of On-line Dictionaries
http://www.yourdictionary.com/

Particularly useful is

OneLook Dictionaries
http://www.onelook.com/
which provides a search of over 600 general and subject dictionaries.

Images

Images on the Net come in a variety of formats, such as gif, jpeg, mpeg, tiff, but some collections may be limited to particular formats. The format of any image you find will determine how you can use it in a web page or file, rather than just printing it. So, for example, a gif image cannot be resized without distorting it.

For an outline of image formats see

Popular image formats
http://www.shortcourses.com/book01/07-03.htm

Typical collections are:

ditto.com
http://www.ditto.com/

Helix
http://www.helix.dmu.ac.uk/
a collection maintained for UK higher education.

Image Finder
http://wuarchive.wustl.edu/

Yahoo! Picture Gallery
http://gallery.yahoo.com/

However, the most comprehensive collections are the huge ones being built up by Microsoft and the Getty organization for commercial purposes. Only a small number of the images are free, but if you have funding for research or project work then you might wish to use these.

Corbis
http://www.corbis.com/

Getty Images
http://www.getty-images.com/

A guide to image collections is provided by the Technical Advisory Services for Images at
http://www.tasi.ac.uk/digital/wsources1.html
or there is Paula Berinstein's

Finding images online
http://www.berinsteinresearch.com/fiolinks.htm

You can also search the web for images – see the multimedia section in Chapter 9.

Images – scientific

Much computer data, such as that from space research, may be received as a digital image or used to generate visual interpretations of results. These images can then be made available on the Internet.

NASA Image Exchange
http://nix.nasa.gov/
A collection of still images of planets, space vehicles, etc.

Latest Hubble Space Telescope Observations
http://www.stsci.edu/pubinfo/Latest.html

Images – medical

Similarly, medical images may be created from various scanning techniques and may be converted into animated or layered images.

Bristol Biomed Image Archive
http://www.brisbio.ac.uk/

Virtual Frog Dissection Kit
http://george.lbl.gov/vfrog/
A three-dimensional representation of the internal structure of a frog with animation and simulation.

The Visible Human
http://www.nlm.nih.gov/research/visible/visible_human.html
http://vhp.gla.ac.uk/
A project to create three-dimensional anatomically detailed representations of the male and female human bodies.

Images – historical and artistic

Paintings, drawings, manuscripts and other traditional forms of image can be put on the Internet to make them widely and easily available. The image quality is, of course, generally poor compared with the original or even with a reproduction in a book.

CGFA: Carol Gerten's Fine Art – a virtual art museum
http://sunsite.org.uk/cgfa/
Paintings from many periods and countries.

Electronic Beowulf
http://www.bl.uk/diglib/beowulf/

Louvre
http://mistral.culture.fr/louvre/
Images of a variety of artforms from the Louvre Museum.

Scottish College of Textiles Gallery
http://www.hw.ac.uk/texWWW/gallery/gallery.html

WebMuseum network
http://sunsite.unc.edu/wm/
Covers a wide range of institutions.

Images – moving/television

There is a growth of video images on the Internet – either to download to disk and play or to view as you connect (so-called 'streaming' video). This includes television news and some educational topics, but much concerns entertainment and has little academic value. Your browser will need a plug-in program to view video. University public IT areas may not allow this.

An example is the US cable TV network C-SPAN with a website:

C-SPAN.org
http://www.c-span.org/
Most of the content is US orientated, but you can see British content such as Prime Minister's Question Time in the House of Commons.

There are a variety of starting points to identify video and television material. They have a US bias.

Current Awareness Resources via Streaming Audio and Video
http://gwis2.circ.gwu.edu/~gprice/audio.htm

EarthStation1
http://www.earthstation1.com/

Internet Television Network
http://intv.net/videolib.htm

Real.com- Guide
http://realguide.real.com/
This links to a European version at **http://europe.real.com/realguide**

Yahoo! Broadcast
http://www.broadcast.com/

One particularly interesting site is

British Pathe News
http://www.britishpathe.com/taste_collection.htm
where a small number of the newsreels from their huge collection can be seen free on the web.

See also Chapter 9 on ways of searching for video images.

Related are web cameras (webcams), which show images from live video cameras, either as poor quality moving images or still images updated every few minutes. Again, much is of a frivolous (and often very boring) nature, but there are some more useful examples. There are lots of urban and rural views that can help with meteorological or air pollution activity and zoologists might find something of interest at

Royal Society for the Protection of Birds
http://www.rspb.org.uk/webcams

The subject collections in Chapter 8 include web camera sites and you can also check at

WebCam Central
http://www.camcentral.com/

Sounds/audio

The Internet may not immediately be thought of as a means of transmitting sounds, but technically it is little different from distributing text or images. (As with video you will also need a browser plug-in to cope with audio.) Listening to radio or downloading CD tracks may not be wholly relevant to your studies but examples of sites that could be more appropriate are:

Current Awareness Resources via Streaming Audio and Video
http://gwis2.circ.gwu.edu/~gprice/audio.htm
Mostly news and current affairs.

EarthStation1
http://www.earthstation1.com
Historical, space archives; sound effects.

Great Speeches
http://www.historychannel.com/speeches/index.html
which has well-known speeches from people like Martin Luther King, Chamberlain and Churchill.

MP3Lit.com
http://www.mp3lit.com
has readings from fiction, poetry, biography etc.

A general guide is

Yahoo! Broadcast
http://www.broadcast.com/

and some of the search services in Chapter 9 cover sounds.

Maps

Digital techniques are widely used in mapping, and digital maps are easily accessed across the Internet. Other maps may simply be used as a visual way of presenting geographical or locational information, for example *World War II Maps* at

http://ac.acusd.edu/History/WW2Index/picindexmapsi.html

You will also find maps incorporated within websites; for example, to show the plan of a university. Complex maps comprise large files which may take a long time to download and display. If you want to reproduce them, you may need a high-resolution printer.

Global Land Information System (GLIS)
http://edcwww.cr.usgs.gov/webglis
Land use maps of the US; graphs/data of geological information.

Magellan Geographix
http://www.maps.com/

Maps of Great Britain on the WWW
http://www.multimap.com/uk/

Mapquest
http://www.mapquest.com/
Search by UK postcode.

Ordnance Survey
http://www.ordsvy.gov.uk/
Includes some maps to download as well as their catalogue.

Perry-Castaneda Library Map Collection
http://www.lib.utexas.edu/Libs/PCL/Map_collection/
Map_collection.html

Your library may subscribe to *EDINA Digimap*, a service for UK higher education providing Ordnance Survey maps at various scales, including urban areas at 1:1250, which also allows the downloading of spatial data for local use.

Useful guides to map collections are:

Maps and References
http://www.cgrer.uiowa.edu/servers/servers_references.html

BUBL LINK Maps
http://link.bubl.ac.uk:80/maps

Numerical data

Data on the Internet can be valuable because it is likely to be more up to date than in printed sources, particularly for any information that changes regularly, and because wide-ranging sources can be brought together. Being electronic, it can be downloaded and easily reused, perhaps in some modelling or manipulation program. However, the range of data available is still limited compared with printed or charged online sources. Remember there is also the *MIMAS* data service described on the previous chapter.

Scientific

Chip Directory
http://www.xs4all.nl/~ganswijk/chipdir/chipdir.html
has property data for electronic components with links to manufacturers' pages.

Physical Reference Data
http://physics.nist.gov/PhysRefData/
Physical constants, nuclear physics, spectral data and more.

Web Elements
http://www.webelements.com/index.html

Physical, chemical and biological property data on the chemical elements.

Economic

Electronic Share Information
http://www.esi.co.uk/
UK share prices and company information, with many shares updated a number of times a day.

Extel Data (selective)
http://www.bized.ac.uk/dataserv/extel/notes/main.htm
Basic financial accounts for 500 leading UK companies.

US Bureau of the Census
http://www.census.gov/
Includes economic as well as demographic data.

Fortune
http://www.pathfinder.com/fortune/
Includes searchable databases (Global 500 and Fortune (US) 500 top companies).

World Income Inequality database
http://www.wider.unu.edu/wiid/wiid.htm
From the UN University World Institute for Development Economics Research.

General statistical

The Data Archive
http://www.data-archive.ac.uk/
Collections of social statistics from UK research. Includes the BIRON catalogue of Economic and Social Research Council material.

Eurostat
http://europa.eu.int/comm/eurostat/

A selection from the European Communities statistical agency.

FEDSTATS
http://www.fedstats.gov
has statistics from 70 US government agencies.

LABSTAT
http://stats.bls.gov/blshome.html
The US Bureau of Labor Statistics public database, which provides current and historical data from 25 surveys.

StatBase
http://www.statistics.gov.uk/statbase/mainmenu.asp
A searchable database of official UK statistics.

Institutional servers

Professional or trade organizations such as the Royal Society of Chemistry or the Institute of Fiscal Studies will have a web presence giving details of their publications, conferences, news, job vacancies, research activity, members, services, Internet links and so on. The web pages for a university department have a similar function.

A collection of such services worldwide is the *Scholarly Societies Project*
http://www.lib.uwaterloo.ca/society/overview.html

Company websites

Commercial companies usually have websites to promote themselves and their products, and increasingly to sell goods across the Internet (what is known as e-commerce). They may include some financial or other information about the company, which would be useful for academic purposes. Many companies now operate only using the web. Some UK examples are:

British Telecom
http://www.bt.com/

Nationwide Building Society
http://www.nationwide.co.uk/

Red or Dead
http://www.redordead.co.uk/

Sainsburys
http://www.sainsburys.co.uk/

You can trace others by using the directories described in Chapter 8 and the search services described in Chapter 9.

Interactive – simulation/control

More imaginative uses of the Internet take advantage of its interactive nature by allowing users to input data or requests and responding to them.

The Bradford Robotic Telescope
http://www.telescope.org/rti
Responds to instructions from users on what to look at and provides them with results.

Exploratorium
http://www.exploratorium.edu/
A collection of electronic exhibits, news and resources for teachers, students and science enthusiasts.

MATTER
http://www.matter.org.uk/
Has various simulations for engineering materials.

Specialist sources

Electronic journals (e-journals)

Thousands of journals, magazines and newsletters are now available on the Internet. Some may look very basic on the screen, having just text, but most are now graphically more adventurous with colour and illustrations. Some are newsletters and fanzines (e-zines) produced by enthusiasts; others are reputable academic journals. Many are the electronic version of a printed journal – and may look exactly the same – but others exist only in electronic format.

Increasingly, established publishers are making available their printed journals as a way of publishing research information more effectively. Access to these is not generally free, but most universities have taken up subscriptions to some of them, so they are free to their staff and students. Publishers involved include Academic Press, Blackwells, Cambridge University Press and Elsevier Science. Many of these journals are available through a number of intermediary suppliers including *ingentaJournals*, *Swetsnet*, *OCLC*, *Infotrac Custom*, *Catchword* and *EBSCO*. Others are available direct from individual publisher's websites. Your library should have a web page listing the publishers concerned, the titles you can view and print and how to get to them. Many will allow access from off-campus.

To find other electronic journals there are various lists:

CIC Consortium
http://ejournals.cic.net/

Scholarly Journals Distributed via the World Wide Web
http://info.lib.uh.edu/wj/webjour.html

University of Pennsylvania
http://www.library.upenn.edu/resources/ej/ej.html

For the wider range of e-zines try the list maintained by John Labovitz at
http://www.meer.net/~johnl/e-zine-list/

Some journals do not appear in complete form on the Internet, but merely offer extracts from the printed journal as a taster: major articles and features, correspondence, book reviews, jobs and so on.

Examples include:

Computer Weekly
http://www.computerweekly.co.uk/

The Economist
http://www.economist.com/

New Scientist
http://www.newscientist.com/

Tables of contents

Even if you aren't able to obtain the full text of particular journals you can often still find out about them, since there are also services giving the table of contents (TOC) – that is, article titles, authors and page numbers – of academic journals. Sometimes there is an abstract (summary) too. You can thus check the contents of the latest issues of specific journals, or often search through back issues and so find out about many journals not stocked in your library to decide whether you want to pursue them further. Some services offer to e-mail you the contents of the latest issue of specified journals, which can be useful if you need to keep up with subjects for research.

Services covering many publishers include:

UnCover
http://uncweb.carl.org/
which provides contents lists from 17,000 current journals.

ingentaJournals
http://www.bids.ac.uk/
has contents from 2500 journals (log in as 'Guest'). However your library may have subscriptions to allow you to get the full text of some of them – in this case login with your *ATHENS* ID.

Catchword
http://pinkerton.bham.ac.uk/

has contents from over 700 UK journals. Again you will have access to the complete text of journals to which your library subscribes.

TOC services from particular publishers include:

Blackwell Science
http://www.blacksci.co.uk/products/journals/jnltitle.htm
Contents of over 200 titles can be viewed.

Elsevier Science
http://www.elsevier.nl/homepage/about/caware/
Journal Tables of Contents provides online tables of contents for more than 1100 journals.

IEEE Xplore
http://ieeexplore.ieee.org/
(Choose 'Tables of Contents'.) Contents from journals, transactions, magazines and conferences from the IEEE (Institute of Electrical and Electronics Engineers) and IEE (Institution of Electrical Engineers).

MCB University Press
http://www.mcb.co.uk/portfolio/home.htm
130 titles, especially in management.

Oxford University Press
http://www3.oup.co.uk/jnls/list/
180 journals in a range of subjects.

Software

There is much software available across the Net – indeed, distributing software was one of the earliest uses of the Internet. The subject guides to Internet resources discussed in Chapter 8 include specialist software collections, and the major software companies like Microsoft have websites which include some free software, such as add-ons and upgrades. However, it may be easier to use sources which cover all subjects and for a variety of hardware platforms. Software available ranges from small utility programs – such as a screen saver, virus checker, HTML editor or decompression program – to large packages such as the Netscape WWW browser, a paint program or a mail system. Although downloading the software is free, some may be 'shareware', that is, you are expected to send the software publisher a small fee to register your use. In return you receive documentation and upgrades. To encourage you to register, the software may become unusable after a prescribed period or a certain date.

UK Mirror Service
http://www.mirror.ac.uk/
is a service for higher education providing software from a variety of sources.

SunSITE Northern Europe
http://src.doc.ic.ac.uk
is one of a number of collections worldwide supported by Sun Microsystems, concentrating on programs for PCs and Unix machines.

Jumbo
http://www.jumbo.com/

and

Shareware.com
http://www.shareware.com/
allow you to search for, browse, and download freeware, shareware, demos, fixes, patches and upgrades from various software archives and computer vendor sites on the Internet.

WinFiles.com
http://www.winfiles.com/
Information and shareware for Windows 95, 98, NT and CE.

A guide to software collections is

Software Directory Directory
http://boole.stanford.edu/nerdsheaven.html

Software can be downloaded to your computer using FTP as outlined in Chapter 4. The *Archie* service mentioned there can also be used to identify named packages from a much wider range of sources.

Newspapers and news services

Most newspapers have a presence on the Net. Usually they offer the main UK and world news, business and sports stories of the day. They may also have comment, letters, arts reviews, and the weather. They can be selective in comparison with the printed newspaper and usually omit photographs and statistical material. On the other hand, they can extend the functions of the printed newspaper by including additional material or setting up discussion forums on particular issues. There is usually a searchable archive of stories. These sites can often be slow to view.

Major British electronic newspaper sites include:

Daily Telegraph
http://www.telegraph.co.uk/

Financial Times
http://www.ft.com/

Guardian/Observer
http://www.guardian.co.uk/

Independent
http://www.independent.co.uk/

Sunday Times
http://www.sunday-times.co.uk/

The Times
http://www.the-times.co.uk/

You may need to register with some of these to get a password. Registration is free and is primarily there for marketing purposes.

UK local newspapers can be traced from **http://www.mediauk. com/** or you can go to **http://www.fish4news.co.uk/** which gathers stories from many local papers. *NISS* links to many UK newspapers at **http://www.niss.ac.uk/cr/uknews.html**

European newspapers on the Internet include:

Der Spiegel
http://www.spiegel.de/

Die Welt
http://www.welt.de/

El Mundo
http://www.el-mundo.es/index.html

Le Monde
http://www.lemonde.fr/

Liberation
http://www.liberation.fr/

You can connect to many of these and others from around the world from *NISS* at

http://www.niss.ac.uk/cr/worldnews.html

A comprehensive list of electronic newspapers published throughout the world is maintained by the US *Editor and Publisher* magazine at

http://www.mediainfo.com/emedia

There are also news services drawing from a number of newspapers or from television news coverage:

Ananova (Press Association*)*
http://www.ananova.com/

BBC News
http://news.bbc.co.uk/

CNN
http://www.cnn.com/

Moreover.com
http://moreover.com/

News Index
http://www.newsindex.com/

NewsNow
http://www.newsnow.co.uk/

Teletext
http://www.teletext.co.uk/

These can include audio or video reports.

Some of these services offer a daily e-mail newsletter summarizing the main stories and often linking to the full story on the web. The *Guardian* has one called The Wrap and you can sign up for others at the *Ananova* and *Moreover* sites.

Reference

The mixture of reference books you find in your library is beginning to be reflected on the Internet. Here we list a few general sources. You can find others at:

DeskRef
http://ansernet.rcls.org/deskref/

Martindale's The Reference Desk
http://www-sci.lib.uci.edu/~martindale/Ref.html

Online Enquiry Desk
http://www.earl.org.uk/earlweb/ref.html
UK orientated.

Refdesk.com
http://www.refdesk.com/

Subject-specific reference books can be traced from the subject collections described in Chapter 8.

For books in general

Internet Book Shop
http://www.bookshop.co.uk/
though primarily an online book ordering service, also includes a database of books currently available in the UK. It is thus useful to search for details of books on a particular subject, whether you intend to buy or not.

The commonest English dictionary available is

Websters Dictionary
http://www.m-w.com/netdict.htm

but there are guides to others, including those in other languages, at:

A Web of Online Dictionaries
http://www.yourdictionary.com/

OneLook Dictionaries
http://www.onelook.com
provides a search of over 600 general and subject dictionaries.

Travlang's Translating Dictionaries
http://dictionaries.travlang.com/
for foreign languages.

More ambitiously there is a rudimentary translation service offered by

AltaVista: Translations
http://www.altavista.co.uk/content/translate.jsp

Or you can try

Systran
http://www.systransoft.com/

For further help with writing English you might want to use

Roget's Thesaurus
http://www.thesaurus.com/

CIA World Fact Book is not sensitive information about you or classified military details, but economic, political and geographical data about all the countries in the world.
http://www.odci.gov/cia/publications/factbook/index.html

YELL
http://www.yell.com/
has the Electronic Yellow Pages, a film finder, online shopping and business services.

For UK telephone numbers go to
http://www.bt.com/phonenetuk/
For others try

Telephone Directories on the Web
http://www.teldir.com
with links to online telephone and fax directories from around the world. Be aware they are not always up to date.

You can get weather forecasts from the *Meteorological Office* at
http://www.meto.gov.uk/
and from the electronic versions of newspapers noted above.

Media UK Internet Directory
http://www.mediauk.com/directory
has TV, radio, newspaper and magazine addresses and contacts, including e-mail addresses.

For biography try

> *Lives, the Biography Resource*
> http://amillionlives.com/

or

> *World Biographical Index*
> http://www.saur-wbi.de/wbi_eng/main.htm

with 2.4 million short biographies from around the world.

Government

Knowledge of what governments are publishing is important not just for those studying the government and politics of the UK, Europe or elsewhere, but for all subjects that have to be put into a practical 'real world' context, such as social sciences, business, applied sciences and so on. Only more theoretical subjects like philosophy or mathematics may have little need for government or 'official' information.

You can obtain information from governments worldwide on the Net, starting at home with the *Open.gov.uk* site at

http://www.open.gov.uk/

This is a gateway to government servers and has material from central government departments and ministries, agencies like the Building Research Establishment and National Rivers Authority, regulatory bodies, projects such as the Private Finance Initiative, museums and quangos. There is also material from local and regional government, charities and the police.

On this site you will typically find lots about the various organizations as well as:

★ consultative documents
★ lists of publications
★ press releases on various developments
★ newsletters and circulars
★ programmes of activities

★ service standards and charters
★ explanatory booklets
★ other publications which are usually free in their printed version
★ selections from priced publications such as statistical returns.

You can look at a department's material, browse subject categories like housing or heritage, or search the full text of the service.

Despite the URL, don't expect to find everything! Though provision is improving, the UK government still needs to sell much of its information, so the useful content is limited. However, there are some other full-text publications, such as Acts of Parliament and White Papers, at

UK Official Publications on the Internet
http://www.official-documents.co.uk/menu/ukpinf.htm

and

ukstate.com
http://www.ukstate.com/
is a new site beginning to make more official information available.

Nevertheless, your library should have a much wider range of government information in print form and you can use the Internet to find out what recent publications it might have if it subscribes to *BOPCAS* at

http://www.soton.ac.uk/~bopcas
which is a frequently updated listing of new publications from the official government publishers, and from government departments themselves. It is based on the stock of Southampton University Library and covers material published since July 1995.

The European Union has a number of services:

Europa
http://europa.eu.int/

has details of EU institutions, speeches, policy documents, statistics and more.

CORDIS
http://www.cordis.lu/
is the Community Research and Development Information Service promoting EU Research & Development activity, with details of projects and publications.

Though not a free resource, your library may have access to

European AccessPlus
http://www.europeanaccess.co.uk/home/home.htm
which has the full text of many EC documents.

In the USA there is a strong emphasis on freedom of information and open government, recognizing that as the public funds government it is entitled to see the resulting information. So there is

FedWorld
http://www.fedworld.gov/
which draws together databases and bulletin boards from 150 agencies. These are useful if you need to examine US practice, but they also have more broadly useful technical and statistical data from bodies such as the Environmental Protection Agency, the Food and Drug Administration and the US Patent Office. There are various databases of publications and a list of government job vacancies.

A comprehensive guide to information sources on government in the US (and elsewhere) is maintained at the University of Texas at
http://www.lib.utexas.edu/Libs/PCL/Government.html

For information on ministries, embassies, local councils and law courts in over 200 countries consult

Governments on the WWW
http://www.gksoft.com/govt/

For access to web servers from national parliaments around the world, try:

Web Sites on National Parliaments
http://www.polisci.umn.edu/information/parliaments/index.
  html

Library catalogues

The most important source of local information will be the catalogue of your own library. Computer-based library catalogues are often referred to as OPACs (online public access catalogues), and an increasing number have web interfaces too. Your own catalogue is likely to be available locally from anywhere on your campus network.

Always check how much of the library's stock is available on the OPAC – some long-established university libraries do not list their older books on the OPAC, and you may have to refer to a card or microfiche catalogue to check this material. Most catalogues will also list the periodicals taken.

The Internet will allow you to search other OPACs from your own institution. There are various reasons why you might wish to do this:

★ to check for books and journals from another local academic library. Usually a university or college library will allow students from other local institutions to consult or photocopy material, though some may limit access during term time. Your own library will advise on what facilities are available, or you may be able to find this information on the web pages of the institution whose library you plan to visit.

★ to check a library you wish to use elsewhere in the country, for example, during vacations or on placement.

★ to search the catalogue of a library that specializes in a topic that you are studying, in order to identify useful sources. For example, if you are studying American or Australian literature, you might wish to search the OPACs of the Library of Congress or the National Library of Australia.

★ to search major copyright libraries, which receive copies of all new books published in the UK.

Please note that if you locate books that you wish to borrow in other libraries, your library will normally borrow them through the British Library's Document Supply Centre, rather than going directly to the library whose OPAC you have searched.

NISS
http://www.niss.ac.uk/lis/opacs.html
provides access to most British academic library catalogues, in addition to some in other countries. You should check the **[Info]** box before connecting to an OPAC, as it often contains useful information on the coverage of the OPAC and whether there are commands needed to log off from the service – it is sometimes easy to get stranded without knowing how to log off.

The British Library's catalogue is at
http://opac97.bl.uk/
and covers books, periodicals, reports and conferences in all its libraries from 1980, and in some cases earlier.

COPAC
http://copac.ac.uk/copac/
is the beginning of a 'national OPAC' service based on the union catalogue database of the Consortium of University Research Libraries (CURL). COPAC currently gives access to the combined library catalogues from 18 universities, including Cambridge, Edinburgh, Glasgow, Leeds and Oxford, with the catalogues of a further five to be added. The service provides search, retrieve, display and download facilities, and is under continual development.

Another listing of UK catalogues – and, more importantly, those from the USA and other countries – is the *Hytelnet* service. This gives access details of catalogues, and also allows telnet access to them and to databases and other services too. *Hytelnet* is at

http://www.lights.com/hytelnet

Teaching and learning material

All the material discussed in this book is included for its value for learning purposes, particularly in providing facts, information, opinions and so on. However, there is also course material with a specifically educational role that gives a structured, guided, and maybe interactive, view of a topic, usually comprising some of the following:

★ lecture notes
★ case studies
★ summaries
★ illustrations
★ video clips
★ simulation
★ animation
★ tests
★ assignments
★ support by e-mail
★ links to useful information.

Typical examples are

Cameron Balloons Virtual Factory
http://bized.ac.uk/virtual/cb/

Course Resources on the Web: Resources for the Teaching of Social Psychology
http://www.noctrl.edu/~ajomuel/crow/

Jackson Pollock 1912–1956
http://www.nga.gov/feature/pollock/pollockhome.html

Online Biology Book
http://gened.emc.maricopa.edu/bio/bio181/BIOBK/
   BioBookTOC.html

Quality Manufacturing Lab
http://www.engr.stmarytx.edu/manufacturing/qm.htm

In some cases there may be complete courses, perhaps offered to anyone who wishes to sign up or designed for specific institutions, but able to be used by others. It is possible that your own courses may use material specially prepared in this way – for all or part of a unit or module – or that you will be referred to some other college's online course. However, it is more likely that you will simply want to look around to see if there is anything that could be used to supplement your own course material. You might find useful background information, such as guidance on using particular computer systems or software, or you may prefer the self-paced learning possible with computer-based material.

There are collections of such material which are arranged in broad subject areas and have some description of the content. The largest of these is the *World Lecture Hall* at the University of Texas
   http://www.utexas.edu/world/lecture/
and there is a similar one – *Teaching and Learning on the WWW* – at Maricopa Community Colleges
   http://www.mcli.dist.maricopa.edu/tl/index.html
The subject collections described in Chapter 8 will include this sort of teaching material.

Most of these courses are from the USA, so they are not always relevant to the UK context, and transatlantic network congestion can sometimes make their use slow and frustrating.

A development in the USA is for companies to employ students to take notes of lectures and then make them available on the web. Examples are

http://www.StudentU.com/classnotes/default.asp

and

http://www.study247.com/

However, these relate to particular US universities so should not be relied upon in your circumstances, or indeed perhaps for their accuracy – they should only be considered as possibly providing some information to supplement your own course material.

Then, of course there are the sites providing ready made assignments and essays, but we wouldn't dream of telling you where they are! Just be aware that academic staff have ways of checking if you have used them.

7

Other student information

★ Study skills
★ Computer skills
★ Placements
★ Overseas study
★ Jobs
★ Travel
★ Welfare
★ Accommodation
★ Student sites

As a student you may also need information other than for the subjects you are studying, so this chapter suggests some sources to help with study skills, finding placements, job hunting, welfare, finance and so on.

Study skills

Its true to say that good skills in studying can be learned and though you may have had some help in the past you might still welcome some further guidance.

There are lots of general sites such as:

Learning Strategies
http://www.muskingum.edu/~cal/database/genpurpose.
html

Managing Your Study
http://io.newi.ac.uk/ISS/study_centre/managing/managing.htm

Study Skills Survival Guide
http://www.sbu.ac.uk/caxton/survival.html

Study Skills Self-help Information
http://www.ucc.vt.edu/stdysk/stdyhlp.html

More specific topics are also covered such as:

Time Management: Making it Work for You
http://www.uoguelph.ca/csrc/learning/lasttm.htm

THINKS: Tutorial Help In Numeracy Key Skills
http://www.qmark.com/questionbank/thinks.html

Grammar Handbook
**http://www.english.uiuc.edu/cws/wworkshop/grammarmenu.
  htm**

Indispensible Writing Resources
http://www.stetson.edu/~rhansen/writing.html

Some directories of such resources include:

Study Guides and Strategies
http://www.iss.stthomas.edu/studyguides/
which deals with preparing to learn, reading skills, taking tests,
writing essays, etc.

Virtual pamphlets
**http://www.cf.ac.uk/uwcc/engin/news/feedback/vpamphlets.
  html**
which link to hundreds of sources on study skills and welfare problems.

Computer skills

Another area that affects most students these days is the need to use computers for documents, data manipulation and information seeking. Your local computing service will provide some guidance, support, documentation and training for the various services and packages you use, but because of the huge increase in computer use by students in the last few years it may not be able to cope with all the demand. However, you can also look elsewhere for help.

You can check your skills at

Basic IT skills checklist
http://www.st-and.ac.uk/ITS/newuser/chklst.html.gz

For most major software you can find guides and tutorials online. For example:

Microsoft Windows
http://www.hum.port.ac.uk/slas/it/windows.htm

Microsoft Word
http://teleeducation.nb.ca/it/module5/word/index.html

Learning Microsoft Access 97
http://cru.cahe.wsu.edu/training/Access97/

Excel Tutorial
http://www.usd.edu/trio/tut/excel/index.html

Internet Explorer 5.0 tutorial
**http://www.recorder.ca/grenvillecap/tutorial/tutorial/
tut-004b1.htm**

Collections of documentation from other universities that you can consult include:

Aberdeen University
http://www.abdn.ac.uk/AUCC/publications/pubslist.htm

Edinburgh University
http://www.ucs.ed.ac.uk/iss/docs/

Leeds University
http://www.leeds.ac.uk/ucs/docs/docs.html

Some of the sites have a search facility. Remember that if the documentation is written for another university, any logon details will not apply to you. You will normally be able to read documentation on the screen, save it into a local file, bookmark it to refer to it later, or print it. However, as a variety of formats are used, including PostScript and Adobe Acrobat, you will only be able to view or print these if your browser is equipped to deal with them.

Another place to look is

help-site.com
http://help-site.com/
which links to various sources of documentation in web format.

As a supplement to documentation you can use the appropriate newsgroups and discussion lists, particularly the **comp** newsgroups, to ask for help from fellow-users. Chapter 3 suggested some ways of identifying particular lists and newsgroups.

Placements

Many courses include a period of placement, varying from a few weeks to a year. Departments are often well organized about recommending suitable placements, but sometimes you will have to find your own. Usually it is necessary to use a directory of companies and organizations for your subject, perhaps with a geographical breakdown. There are not yet many trade directories of this sort on the Internet, but useful general ones include:

CountyWeb
http://www.countyweb.co.uk/
arranged by UK county.

Scoot
http://www.scoot.co.uk/
which claims to be the biggest classified UK business directory on the WWW, with two million entries.

YELL.com
http://www.yell.com/
has the electronic version of BT"s *Yellow Pages*, searchable by location and category.

Europages: the European Business Directory
http://www.europages.com/
has details of 500,000 suppliers from 25 countries. You can search the database by keyword or company name. Contact details and brief business descriptions are given.

Big Yellow
http://www.bigyellow.com/
has contact details of US companies, searchable by industry, name, city.

Some listings for specific industries are in

Subject Trade Directories
http://www.dis.strath.ac.uk/business/trade.html

These directories won't provide much information about the companies, so you may still need to consult printed trade directories or CD-ROM services such as *FAME* in your library. Once you have selected organizations you may be able to find a website for more information using the subject collections described in the next chapter or a search engine for the particular country concerned, as noted in Chapter 9.

Overseas study

You may be spending a term/semester/year in another country, perhaps with the ERASMUS programme:

http://europa.eu.int/comm/education/socrates/erasmus/

The institution to which you are going will doubtless have a web server from which you can get information. You can check for it on the world list of web servers at

http://www.mth.uea.ac.uk/VL/Servers.html

or maybe find the URL more easily from *BRAINTRACK* (page 40) or with one of the search services discussed in Chapter 9.

If you want information on the country you are going to then you can try:

Excite Travel
http://www.excite.com/travel/

Rough Guides
http://www.roughguides.com/

or the *CIA World Fact Book* at
http://www.odci.gov/cia/publications/factbook/index.html

Remember that when you are on placement or studying elsewhere you are likely to have access to e-mail to keep in touch with your university or college.

Jobs

The Internet is becoming an important source of information on job vacancies, both because of the advertisements in the electronic versions of newspapers and specialist magazines, and also because of the growth of specialist websites, which increasingly may be the only place where some vacancies are announced. The recruitment process is quicker, and there are even cases of people being interviewed for overseas jobs by e-mail!

These sites cover a wider range of jobs, though outside the academic area these are often mostly in IT, management and finance. They may advertise vacancies or allow you to submit a CV for recruiters to consider. Not all advertisements are for the permanent full-time job you might be seeking at the end of your course; they may help if you are looking for part-time work during your course or for vacation work.

You can find information about the job seeking process: there are some notes on

Writing a Curriculum Vitae at
http://www.bton.ac.uk/studentserv/how towriteacv.html

You can learn about interviews at

job-interview.net
http://www.job-interview.net/

or do a psychometric test at
http://www.workunlimited.co.uk/Psychometrics/

Many of the sites below have similar information.

For a general guide to the job-hunting process and to further study, with many links to resources, see the University of London's *Job Hunting on the Internet*
http://www.careers.lon.ac.uk/helpshts/webjob.htm

The *NISS* site gives a useful introduction to job vacancies, with lists of those in higher education arranged by subject at
http://www.vacancies.ac.uk/
and jobs from publications like the *New Scientist*, *The Times* and The *Guardian*, and links to services, including some of those noted below at
http://www.niss.ac.uk/cs/careers/recruit.html
Your careers service may have web pages that link to such services too.

Sources for student opportunities – jobs and further courses – include:

ProspectsWeb
http://www.prospects.csu.man.ac.uk/
from the Central Services Unit, which publishes UK job vacancies
in printed form, and has details of employers and help with career
planning; or

GET
http://www.get.co.uk/

Other sites for graduates include:

Activate: the student careers portal
http://www.activatecareers.com/

Gradunet, the On-Line Graduate Recruitment Guide
http://www.gradunet.co.uk/

For temporary jobs try:

fish4jobs
http://www.fish4jobs.co.uk/
which has adverts from local newspapers.

Summer Jobs
http://www.summerjobs.com/

temps1st.com
http://www.temps1st.com/

Hotrecruit
http://www.hotrecruit.co.uk/

Tate Appointments
http://www.tate.co.uk/
'the temp specialist'.

There are a number of general UK recruitment sites (some including temporary jobs), such as:

CVindex
http://www.cvindex.com/

Jobmall
http://www.jobmall.co.uk/

Jobsite UK
http://www.jobsite.co.uk/

Jobsunlimited
http://www.jobsunlimited.co.uk/

People Bank
http://www.peoplebank.com/

Reed Employment
http://www.reed.co.uk/

StepStone
http://www.stepstone.co.uk/

Others specialize in particular areas, such as:

Jobs for the Academic Community
http://www.jobs.ac.uk/

IT Jobs Homepage
http://Internet-Solutions.com/itjobs.htm
with links to many IT recruitment agencies.

jobs4publicsector.com
http://www.jobs4publicsector.com/

Job Serve
http://www.jobserve.com/
for IT.

There are many Usenet newsgroups for jobs including:
alt.jobs; bionet.jobs.offered; biz.jobs.offered; ie.jobs (Ireland);
uk.jobs.offered and **uk.jobs.wanted**

Many others deal with other geographical areas, especially in the USA.

For jobs outside the UK you can use jobs websites from overseas – find them by doing a search on a subject directory like *Yahoo!* (**http://www.yahoo.com/**).

Travel

The Net is a suitable medium to distribute the continually changing information on travel – fares and timetables – and to provide an easy way to book. Some useful sources are:

a2btravel.com
http://www.a2btravel.com/
which has timetables for coach, rail and air services and other travel information.

UK Public Transport Information
http://www.pti.org.uk/
has all types of transport including ferries, metros and trams.

Railtrack
http://www.railtrack.co.uk/travel/
has timetables,

Trainline
http://www.thetrainline.com/
has timetables, ticket prices and booking facilities.

Internet World Travel Guide
http://www.wtg-online.com/
deals with a variety of means of travel.

FCO Travel Advice
http://www.fco.gov.uk/travel/
from the Foreign and Commonwealth Office has advice on foreign countries, especially those to avoid because of political unrest, epidemics etc; medical advice can be found at

Medical Advisory Services for Travellers Abroad
http://www.masta.org/

Exchange rates for major currencies can be found at:
http://www.airwise.com/services/currconv.html
Other travel information sources can be found at
http://www.niss.ac.uk/world/travel/

Welfare

Student life can involve the need for help with finance, health and other problems. Important sources of information for these are the Citizens Advice Bureaux which will exist in most cities and large towns. As well as visiting them you can check online at

Advice Guide
http://www.adviceguide.org.uk/
for topics such as traffic accidents, benefits, electricity bills, credit and so on.
Another resource is

Virtual pamphlets
http://www.cf.ac.uk/uwcc/engin/news/feedback/vpamphlets. html
which has links to hundreds of sources on welfare problems.

For information about student finance see:

Higher Education Student Support
http://www.dfee.gov.uk/support/index.htm
which has various documents from the Department for Education and Employment on the loans system.

Student Loans Company
http://www.slc.co.uk/
with information on loan terms, eligibility, repayments, how to apply and so on. You cannot yet apply through the Internet!

Freefund.com
http://freefund.com/
which is a guide to scholarships and other sources of funding.

If you have personal, health or other problems affecting your work there are many people to talk to, for example tutors, lecturers, friends, student counsellors, chaplains and so on. However, if you find it easier to communicate less directly then you may be able to find appropriate help and information on the Internet.

For health information you can use

NHSDirect
http://www.nhsdirect.nhs.uk/
which has a guide to symptoms and how to treat them and information (including audio files) on various conditions. It supplements the telephone service available in most parts of the UK.

There are many other Internet health sites, such as

Patient UK
http://www.patient.co.uk/
though these don't necessarily replace a visit to a doctor.

If you have access to *Usenet* then there are numerous newsgroups in the **alt.support** hierarchy dealing with topics such as diet, depression, loneliness, learning disabilities and various medical problems.

There is a useful guide called *Emotional Support on the Internet* that lists pertinent newsgroups and discussion lists. It is issued regularly on many relevant newsgroups as a FAQ and is also available at:

http://faqs.org/faqs/support/emotional/resources-list/
The Samaritans can be found at

http://www.samaritans.org.uk/

Accommodation

The accommodation services at many universities use the institutional websites to publish lists of vacancies. Access may be limited to that particular university. In some cases the service is a joint one between universities in the same city.

Student sites

An increasing number of student-orientated websites cover welfare, finance, job hunting as well as music, sport, cinema, drinking and other subjects of importance to the student experience. Some style themselves as magazines, but all have a similar approach:

4-D
http://www.4-d.co.uk/

Juiced
http://www.juiced.co.uk/

National Union of Students
http://www.nus.org.uk/

Red Mole
http://www.redmole.co.uk/

The Site
http://www.thesite.org.uk/
for all young people.

Student Magazine
http://www.studentmagazine.com/

Student-net
http://www.student-net.co.uk/
includes local information.

Student UK
http://www.studentuk.com/

StudentZone
http://www.studentzone.org.uk/

Many individual universities also have student websites, either as web only or relating to the campus newspaper, for example:

Exepose at the University of Exeter
http://gosh.ex.ac.uk/

Hullfire at Hull University
http://www.hull.ac.uk/php/hullfire/

Varsity Online at Cambridge University
http://www.varsity.cam.ac.uk/

8

Browsing for subject information

★ Academic multidisciplinary subject directories
  UK
  Non-UK
★ General subject directories (portals)
★ Subject gateways and hubs
  Resource Discovery Network
★ Subject resource guides

There are two main ways to track information on the Internet: using a search engine or other retrieval tool (see Chapter 9), or browsing in an Internet subject directory or gateway, which this chapter deals with. Parallel with the development of more sophisticated Internet retrieval tools have been attempts to organize the Internet intellectually. In response to the need for better subject access to Internet resources, various services have been set up to facilitate this – the major ones are discussed in this chapter.

The earliest collections of resources organized by subject were known as subject trees. These offered a method of organizing related resources without regard to their physical location, and normally include direct links to the listed resources. Nowadays they are usually referred to as *subject gateways*, subject collections or *directories*, and may either be multidisciplinary or focus on a particular subject area. They are ideally suited to browsing for information, when you wish to know what resources are available in a specific subject area.

The subject gateways tend to evaluate and describe Internet resources, but other services simply add links to hierarchical menus (sometimes known as 'channels'). An increasing number of websites have developed the *portal* concept – incorporating a directory of Internet sites along with news feeds, free e-mail and other tools. A portal can be a valuable starting point in an unfamiliar subject area or for new Internet users, but the impetus for development is usually commercial and supported by advertising.

Portals are intended as a one-stop shop or department store to keep users at that site viewing the adverts or using the shopping facilities. They have limitations for individuals who may want to develop their own resource collections using local web pages and bookmarks (see Chapter 4) as well as portals. Portals can be slow to load and may be poorly designed. Home pages for the major consumer-oriented Internet Service Providers (eg Freeserve, Virgin.net) are portals.

Traffick: the Guide to Portals
http://www.traffick.com/
follows web portal trends with regular columns, news, comparisons, tools, tutorials, specialized reports and statistics.

Academic multidisciplinary subject directories

The sites below include an element of annotation – with brief descriptions or reviews of resources, rather than mere links.

UK subject directories

BUBL Link
http://www.bubl.ac.uk/Link/
is a long-established project that selects, organizes and describes high-quality resources of academic relevance.

Non-UK subject directories

AlphaSearch

http://www.calvin.edu/library/searreso/internet/as/
provides instant access to hundreds of gateway sites. It offers both searching and browsing facilities by discipline and/or resource type. All sites included in *AlphaSearch* have been evaluated on content, academic appropriateness and currency.

InfoMine

http://lib-www.ucr.edu/
offers searching and browsing in its collection of over 16,000 academically valuable resources in a whole range of subject areas. Internet resources include databases, electronic journals, electronic books, bulletin boards, listservs, online library catalogs, articles and directories of researchers.

Scout Report Signpost

http://www.signpost.org/signpost/
contains Internet resources chosen by the editorial staff of the *Scout Report* (a series of electronic newsletters listing new resources) at

http://www.ilrt.bris.ac.uk/mirrors/scout/report/sr/about.html
which have been cataloged and organized for efficient browsing and searching.

Top of the Web

http://www.december.com/web/top.html
John December nominates his 'top five' resources in the following categories: art, business, computers, education, entertainment, government, humanities, keywords, lookup, marketing, money, news, people, science, software and subjects.

The World Wide Web Virtual Library was the first subject-based collection of web resources, predating the development of graphical browsers for the world wide web. It is a distributed subject catalogue, created by volunteers from around the world, who are often experts in their own field. Note that it does not cover all subject

areas. The URL for the UK mirror site is
http://www.mth.uea.ac.uk/VL/Home.html
but you will find that specific subject sections are based wherever
they are maintained.

General subject directories (portals)

The resources below tend to include a search facility (see Chapter
9) in addition to the opportunity to browse by subject. This search
facility may be restricted to directory entries in the portal, or may
cover the whole web. To use these services to their full potential, it
is important to read any Help or Information files that are provided. These will tend to discuss search strategies, Boolean syntax, and
any personalization options offered.

About.com
http://home.about.com/index.htm
is a network of sites including over 700 highly targeted 'environ-
ments' or subject areas, with annotations. Many leisure areas are covered, and the section on Internet/online is valuable for beginners.

Britannica.com
http://www.britannica.com/
lets users simultaneously search the complete, updated *Encyclopaedia
Britannica* with reviews of more than 125,000 websites, articles from
leading magazines, and related books.

EARLweb
http://www.earl.org.uk/earlweb/index.html
is a ready reference to information on the Internet for public library
staff. However, the sections on lifelong learning, science and technology, the citizen in society, imagination and memory, the online
enquiry desk, and business intelligence are of wider interest.

Excite UK
http://www.excite.co.uk/
is a large database of Internet resources, which offers two approach-

es to locating information: a search facility and channels, which are organized by topic in a many-tiered hierarchy.

Galaxy
http://www.einet.net/galaxy.html
provides ten subject categories, each with subheadings, to browse.

Looksmart UK
http://www.looksmart.co.uk/
provides keyword search, a category-based directory and interactive search services.

Lycos UK
http://www.lycos.co.uk/
provides a browsable directory (webguides) and a range of search options. Lycos provides users with subsidized software tools to filter out offensive content.

Magellan
http://magellan.excite.com/
is an online directory with brief annotations about each resource listed in its 18 browsable subject categories.

UK Directory
http://www.ukdirectory.com/
aims to provide a comprehensive guide to everything in the UK on the web.

UK Index
http://www.ukindex.co.uk/index.html
does not offer a browsing facility, but the search facility can be combined with category searching and brief summaries of resources are provided.

WebCrawler
http://webcrawler.com/
is a search tool that also offers 19 channels for browsing Internet resources.

Yahoo! UK &Ireland
http://uk.yahoo.com/
is frequently talked about as a search tool, but it is more accurately described as a virtual library or directory. Users can search the database to find information on the web, or browse down *Yahoo!*'s 14 hierarchical categories.

Subject gateways and hubs

Subject gateways collect and evaluate Internet resources in a particular subject area. The majority of these included here were created to help students (and staff) identify quality resources relevant to their studies, and are included in the *World Wide Web Virtual Library* (see page 116). A number of the Internet resources listed below are included in *Pinakes*, a website which aims to catalogue major subject gateways:

http://www.hw.ac.uk/libWWW/irn/pinakes/pinakes.html

The majority of the gateways listed below aim to provide a comprehensive list of relevant UK-based sources in their subject area, as well as a guide to high-quality international networked resources. Such gateways normally evaluate, select and describe the resources they include and in many cases it is possible to browse the resource descriptions before connecting directly to the resource itself. A search facility, allowing keyword searching of the descriptions and other information, is normally available. Most of these sites will also include a 'what's new' facility, background information on the project, and possibly additional subject services.

These gateways were mostly developed in the second half of the 1990s, and during 2000 many of them will be incorporated into the *Resource Discovery Network* (see below). Some of the most important subject gateways are listed below:

ADAM – art, design, architecture & media
http://adam.ac.uk/

AERADE – aerospace and defence
http://aerade.cranfield.ac.uk/

BIOME – health and life sciences
http://biome.ac.uk/
(incorporating *OMNI* – http://omni.ac.uk/)

Biz/ed – economics and business
http://www.bizednet.bris.ac.uk/

Business Information Sources on the Internet
http://www.dis.strath.ac.uk/business/index.html

CAIN – conflict studies
http://cain.ulst.ac.uk/

Chemdex – chemistry
http://www.chemdex.org/

EEVL – engineering
http://eevl.ac.uk/

ELDIS – development and the environment
http://nt1.ids.ac.uk/eldis/

History
http://ihr.sas.ac.uk/

Humbul – humanities
http://www.humbul.ac.uk/

Lingu@NET – language learning
http://www.linguanet.org.uk/

Port – maritime studies
http://www.port.nmm.ac.uk/

psi-com – public understanding of science
http://www.psci-com.org.uk/

RUDI – urban design
http://rudi.herts.ac.uk/

SOSIG – social sciences, business and law
http://sosig.ac.uk/

Resource Discovery Network

The *Resource Discovery Network (RDN)*
http://www.rdn.ac.uk/
is a UK resource being developed to carry forward the subject gateway concept. It should simplify access to these gateways and will cover academic subjects according to faculty hub, with a number of subject gateways clustered round each hub. Most *RDN* hubs will be launched during 2000.

Subject resource guides

In addition to gateways, directories and portals which provide links to websites in a particular subject area, there have been many guides created which describe the full range of Internet resources (websites, discussion lists, newsgroups, FTP archives, etc.) for a specific topic. These guides will normally include annotations or comments, and are particularly valuable if the author is an authority on the topic. If a guide has been produced for a topic of interest to you, then much of the preliminary browsing has already been done – provided that the guide is comprehensive and is kept up-to-date!

The major collection of these guides is the *Argus Clearinghouse*
http://www.clearinghouse.net/

Unfortunately, guides are not available for every subject area and in some cases are merely lists of discussion lists. One useful feature of the *Argus Clearinghouse* is that it provides the date on which a guide was last updated and contact details for the author.

9

Searching for information

★ Boolean and other concepts for searching
★ Searching the web
★ Searching discussion lists and newsgroup message archives
★ Search tool collections

Searching is a key approach to using the Internet, but in some circumstances it may not be appropriate: browsing sources as discussed in the previous chapter is often more fruitful. It is not possible to 'search the Internet' in the sense of easily searching everything there is: it is more a matter of searching various parts.

Thus you might search:

★ some millions of the available web pages using the general web search engines
★ discussion list archives
★ Usenet newsgroup archives
★ e-mail address directories
★ subject databases like the *BIDS* and *FirstSearch* collections
★ individual websites, such as the *Government Information Service* or a particular university's site
★ reference sources, such as a business directory or an encyclopedia
★ Usenet FAQs

★ software archives and indexes like *Archie*
★ archives of data or images.

Some of these have been noted in previous chapters, so this chapter will concentrate on some principles and the more general services that find textual information on the web.

Concepts

To use any of these search facilities you need to understand the main concepts used. You may be familiar with some of these if you have searched CD-ROMs or other electronic databases in your library.

Boolean logic

Of most importance in searching is the use of AND, OR and NOT (Boolean logic).

★ Use AND to join concepts to make a search more specific. You want *all* the words to be present, eg oil AND pollution AND north AND sea
★ Use OR to widen the search when you want *any* of a set of words to be present, or to specify synonyms, eg marine OR ocean OR sea
★ Use NOT to *exclude* words, eg pollution NOT air.

You can create more complex searches by using brackets, eg oil AND pollution AND (sea OR ocean OR marine).

Some search facilities may ask you to enter search terms (or keywords) in a box without making clear whether it will use AND or OR in searching, so you need to find out first. Some services require you to type AND or OR, others to indicate if you want 'all words' or 'any words' by checking (clicking) a box or by choosing from a menu. Some use + or – as alternative commands.

Search tips

The ability to search on part of a word so as to find material on similar words can simplify searching. So 'medic' (maybe input as medic%, medic? or medic*) will find material containing 'medical' or 'medicine'. This process is known as truncation, word stemming or using a wildcard.

Fields

For large databases or textual material it is useful if you can restrict your search to a particular part (or field) of the information on the database, such as the document title, the summary (or abstract), index terms, or the URL for Internet resources, in order to get more accurate results. So if you are just trying to find a URL for a particular organization, for example, limiting the search on the organization's name to the URL field should give a more rapid result. Specialist databases might have other choices, so a software database would allow the selection of a specific operating system and a yellow pages or phone directory might need a particular location.

Entering terms

Many services are searching very large databases – those for the web are looking through millions of pages – so any words you look for may appear many times. While a search for an uncommon name would probably find a small number of useful items, it is not a good idea to look for a single common term such as 'AIDS' or 'global warming' without being more precise unless you are willing to plough through thousands of references. You would also usually find references containing the word 'aids'. In such instances a subject collection as described in the previous chapter may be more useful. Conversely having too many search terms might produce nothing, when a slightly broader search could be helpful.

The context of the words you want may be wrong too, so a

search for 'Craig Bruce' or 'Craig AND Bruce' might find Bruce
Craig or a document that refers to, say, Bill Bruce and Craig someone else. However, some services do include a NEAR command to
find words that are close together, and more often you can search
for phrases, either by enclosing the words in quotation marks (" ")
or by checking a box for this option.

Don't forget to consider alternative words or phrases. Thus, if
you wanted to find out about fibre optics (used for computer and
telephone network cables), you would need to take account of the
US spelling 'fiber' and the phrase 'optical fibres' which is also used.

Natural language

Some services are starting to offer natural language input so that
users don't have to take account of Boolean terms or + but merely
say what they want and the search software translates this into a
query. The interpretation is not always correct, but sometimes the
system may respond with a need for clarification, eg Which
Washington do you want? A good example of natural language
input is the *Ask Jeeves* web search service (**http://www.ask.co.uk/**).

Scoring of results

Some web search programs rank the search results with a scoring
mechanism based on the placing of the keywords and their fre-
quency, assuming that a document will be more relevant if the
words appear in its title or frequently throughout the pages rather
than occuring once at the end of the document. The results of your
search will be displayed with the highest scoring first – maybe
showing a numerical value with a maximum of 1.0, 1000 or 100%
or a star grading with maybe a maximum of 4. This process is not
always effective, however, so do not assume that only the first 10 or
20 sources retrieved will be of value. You may need to look further
through the list or reformulate your search to be more precise.
Moreover different techniques are used by different services so a

high ranked site in one service may be much lower in others.

Unfortunately you cannot assume that because you know how to use one service you can use the others – often services have their own way of doing things! Thus, when using a search facility, you should read the instructions carefully, preferably before entering the search terms. The instructions may be on the search screen, or you may have to look for a 'help', 'info', 'about', 'tips' or 'instructions' option that calls up detailed guidance, maybe with examples.

Searching the web

The general web search tools (alternatively called search programs, search services or search engines) are frequently assumed to be the starting point to find information on the Internet. Often they are, but at other times a subject directory like *Yahoo!* or *BUBL LINK* or a specialist resource may be more appropriate. These services are limited in that they cannot search FTP archives, message archives, subject databases, library catalogues or services available by telnet, but may include Usenet groups. Other services will search these resources.

The world wide web is an ever-growing collection of information, unstructured compared with a bibliographic database and there is no clearly defined 'web' for these services to search. They each create their own version of the web by using 'robot' or 'crawler' programs. These start from a basic list of web sources and follow the hyperlinks to other sources, recording details of the pages they find in a database. Different starting points and robots that work in different ways, mean that the databases created are different in content. None is comprehensive in its coverage – the largest indexes only about half of the available estimated one billion pages – and there is overlap between them. Similarly there are differences in the way these databases are indexed and searched. This explains why different search services do not give the same results in response to a given search request. It is thus important to look at any help files to see how the services work and how to use them.

They are most effective when searching for a precise term, like the name of a person or organization, though a common name would need to be associated with a narrowing concept too.

Most databases have a fairly basic search, which might have some Boolean options, but there is usually a further page – maybe labelled 'Power' or 'Advanced' search with fuller Boolean, field searching and so on. Since they base searching mainly on words in the text of web pages, rather than on a specialist index, services are likely to return hundreds (or even thousands) of items unless you try to be precise in what you look for. Even then you will still get some wholly irrelevant results. However, search engines are developing new techniques to move away from word searching. Some try to take account of the popularity of sites and return a Top Ten of most-requested sites to a query, or rank highest sites with the most links. *Google* (**http://www.google.com/**) does this. In other services website owners can pay for their site to be displayed first.

Examples

There are many different search services and their features and size vary – what has the greatest coverage when this book is written may well not have by the time you read it – and there is never any 'best' one. At present the most useful ones are probably:

AltaVista
http://www.altavista.co.uk/

Excite
http://www.excite.co.uk/

FAST
http://www.alltheweb.com/

Google
http://www.google.com/

Hotbot
http://www.hotbot.com/

Infoseek
http://infoseek.go.com/

Lycos
http://www.lycos.co.uk/

Northern Light
http://www.northernlight.com/

Their key features are shown in Table 9.1, which can also be found at
http://www.unn.ac.uk/features.htm

There are possibly a billion pages on the web but no service at the time of writing (June 2000) has more than around 300 million pages. *Northern Light* also has a database of electronic journal articles, but you have to pay to retrieve the full text of these. Most of the services have other searchable sources, such as e-mail addresses (noted in Chapter 3) and yellow pages, a subject directory of resources and other features like news and online shopping.

They are trying to be the only entry point – or 'portal' – to the Internet that a user needs, just as ISPs like Freeserve do too. Some of the latter services incorporate these major search services, so Virgin.net uses *Google*. You may find you prefer one or two over the others, especially if you just want 'something' on a subject, or if you need to use a particular search feature. However, for an effective search – to find a very precise piece of information or to find as much as possible – you will need to use a number of them.

Notes: see over

Table 9.1 Features of web search services

	AltaVista	Excite	FAST	Google	Hotbot	Infoseek	Lycos	Northern Light
Other sources	*Usenet*, sounds, pictures	*Usenet*, news, e-mail addresses	Multimedia (from *Lycos*)	None	*Usenet*, sounds, pictures	*Usenet*, e-mail addresses, pictures	Sounds, pictures	Journal articles
Implied OR, AND	Implied OR	Implied OR	Implied AND	Implied AND	Implied AND	Implied OR	Implied AND	Implied AND
Uses + and –	Yes	Yes	No	Yes	Yes	Yes	Yes	Yes
Uses AND, OR, NOT	In Advanced Search	Yes	Yes (menu)	No	Yes	No	Yes	Yes
Fields	title, URL, text	No	domain, language	No	title, domain, etc	title, URL, etc	URL, title, text, etc	title, text, URL, etc
	Uses title:		Uses title: and from menu		Uses title: or from menu	Uses title: or from menu	Uses title: or from menu	Uses title: or from menu
Truncation	Uses *	No	No	No	Uses *	No	No	Uses *
Adjacency (phrase)	Uses " "	Uses " "	From menu	Uses " "	Uses " " or from menu	Uses " "	Uses " " or from menu	Uses " "
Proximity	Uses NEAR	No	No	No	No	No	Uses NEAR	No

Notes

'Other sources'. The service may search other Internet sources as well as the world wide web pages: most commonly the message archives of Usenet newsgroups. Many also link to services providing e-mail address directories, company information, and so on, and may have a directory of Internet resources arranged by subject.

'Implied OR, AND'. Search words will be automatically OR'd together to look for pages with **any** of the words or AND'd to look for pages containing **all** of them.

'Uses + and –'. Terms that must be present can be prefixed with + (the 'require' symbol). Those that must not be present can be indicated with – ('reject' symbol).

'Uses AND, OR, NOT'. Terms can be linked with these Boolean operators as described above. Some services have options, such as 'all these words', 'any of these words' with the same purpose.

'Adjacency'. Specify that words must be next to each other, as in a phrase or person's name.

'Proximity'. Ensure that search words are near each other, eg in the same sentence or within a certain number of words.

Metasearch services

These are services that search most of the general services from one search screen so that you can avoid having to connect to lots of them. They include:

Dogpile
http://www.dogpile.com/

Metacrawler
http://www.metacrawler.com/

Mamma
http://www.mamma.com/

They can be fast, compared with searching services separately, but may have limits on the number of items returned from each service. The common search screen means you do not have the flexibility of searching offered when using the different services directly. They are best for single word or phrase searches.

Regional services

The general web search services above are all US-based – some with UK addresses – and though they do have a worldwide coverage they tend to be dominated by US sources. If you want a more limited coverage geographically – say to find the URL for a German university or information that must relate to Britain – then a UK or European service may have a better coverage or simply be easier to use. These services are limited to the country domain in a web address, eg **.uk**, so will not pick up sites using the international **.com** domain. The major examples are:

Mirago
http://www.mirago.co.uk/

Search UK
http:// searchuk.com/

UKMax
http://www.ukmax.com/

EuroFerret
http://www.euroferret.com/

Euroseek
http://www.euroseek.net/

For other countries see the geographically arranged list at
http://bubl.ac.uk/searches/countries/

or

Regional search engines
http://searchenginewatch.internet.com/links/Regional_Search _Engines/

Multimedia

A growing number of services now offer a facility to search the web for sound files and images. These are not always accurate for images, because most have to search for words in captions, web page titles and the text of pages containing the image, since there is rarely any accurate description of the image to use.

General services like *AltaVista*, *Hotbot*, *Infoseek*, *Lycos* and *Mamma* have options for sounds and pictures and specialist ones include:

Ditto.com
http://ditto.com/

Yahoo! Image surfer
http://isurf.yahoo.com/
for still pictures.

WebSEEk
http://disney.ctr.columbia.edu/webseek
for still pictures and video.

Whoopie!
http://www.whoopie.com/
for audio and video.

These also allow you to browse by subject.

Subject search services

There are an increasing number of services that search only web pages in particular subject areas, for example:

The Academic Directory
http://acdc.hensa.ac.uk/
for UK higher educational sources.

SearchEdu.com
http://www.searchedu.com/
for US higher educational sources.

Artsearch
http://www.artsearch.net/

Energysearch
http://www.energysearch.com/

Law Crawler
http://www.lawcrawler.com/

Mathsearch
http://www.maths.usyd.edu.au:8000/MathSearch.html

Medical World Search
http://www.mwsearch.com/

UK Engineering Search Engine
http://www.eevl.ac.uk/uksearch.html

Others can be found in the subject gateways noted in Chapter 8 and in the search tool collections listed below. Some are included in

Specialty Search Engines
http://www.searchenginewatch.com/links/Specialty_Search_
  Engines/

Newsgroups and discussion lists

Though discussion list and newsgroup messages might seem ephemeral, they are normally stored for a while, and can be a valuable source of up-to-date practical information and news. There are various ways to search archives for many of these, though unfortunately not for all discussion lists.

The UK *Mailbase* service
http://www.mailbase.ac.uk/
keeps two year's messages for each of its lists. These can be browsed and specific lists or groups of lists can be searched. The archives allow direct connection to any Internet sources quoted in messages. Extensive documentation is available.

Lists using the *Listserv* mailing program allow a batch search of archives – that is, you send a message with your search requirement and receive an e-mail response. When you join such a list you will receive instructions on searching.

Some of these lists have web archives of messages that you can browse and search, and again you will be informed if this is so when you subscribe.

The archives of newsgroups can be searched using various web services. Long established is

Deja.com
http://www.deja.com/usenet

and equally useful is

RemarQ
http://www.remarq.com/

A Usenet option is also offered by a number of the web search services discussed in the previous section (see Table 9.1). All these services can have different search facilities, and you need to check their 'help' files to see how much of Usenet is covered and how far back they search.

The FAQs included in many newsgroups were mentioned in Chapter 3.

Search tool collections

There are various collections of search services you can use that can make it easier to remember what is available. They usually link to general and subject web search services and e-mail address directories, and maybe to subject collections, software archives and 'what's new' services too. Sometimes, however, they are just long lists that may confuse you, and they often give insufficient guidance on the use of services.

Graphical browsers used to access the web usually have a search option like Netscape's 'Net Search' and Internet Explorer's 'Go/Search the web' buttons that link to the search services noted here and usually to others too.

General

Search Centre
http://www.tka.co.uk/search
has a business focus and covers web pages, files, software and people.

BIG Search Engine Index
http://www.search-engine-index.co.uk/
has a large list of over 500 sources covering people, software, images and more.

Subject

There are other services that concentrate on identifying the specialist subject databases that are not searched by the general web search services.

Direct Search
http://gwis2.circ.gwu.edu/~gprice/direct.htm
has a huge number of specialist resources, especially in business and politics.

Other with a less academic content are:

Allsearchengines.com
http://www.allsearchengines.com/

The Big Hub
http://www.thebighub.com/

Invisible Web
http://www.invisibleweb.com/

Lycos Searchable Databases
http://dir.lycos.com/Reference/Searchable_Databases/

SearchIQ
http://www.searchiq.com/subjects/

SearchPower
http://www.searchpower.com/

The subject directories in the previous chapter will also direct you to appropriate searchable sources.

10

Keeping up with new resources

* ★ Printed sources
* ★ General sources with a broad coverage
* ★ Selective sources for education
* ★ Specialist sources
    Discussion lists and electronic journals
    Search tools
* ★ Monitoring changes to Internet resources
* ★ Software agents

If you are a regular user of the Internet then it may be important for you to know about new resources quickly, rather than waiting until they reach subject gateways or other directories. For example, you may wish to monitor how businesses are using the Net for an assignment, check out the latest version of software or see who is conducting research in your subject area.

However, keeping up with new resources on the Internet is not easy as many new websites, discussion lists, newsgroups and electronic journals can be created each day. Here we discuss the most useful services that help you to keep up-to-date – you will need to decide which ones will be of most value to you.

The popular UK Internet magazines like *.net* and *Internet Magazine,* and the computing sections of daily newspapers, make some attempt to list new services together with comments, but they can only be very selective in what they include and are not particularly oriented to academic material. The websites for a selection of these magazines are provided in Chapter 13.

The most comprehensive and up-to-date listings of new resources are to be found on the Internet itself. You need to check web-based announcement services regularly for updates, but they have the advantage of offering direct links to the new services listed. Announcement services delivered by e-mail are more convenient, but can clog up your mailbox. You need to be very selective in using these services, as it is possible to spend a vast amount of time just looking at new web pages, some of which may be of very marginal interest. Many quality websites (such as the subject gateways listed in Chapter 8) include a 'What's new' feature to let you know which new links have been added to them in the last week or so; your local university web pages may do likewise. Possibly the most useful round-up of new resources for academic users is Heriot-Watt University's monthly *Internet Resources Newsletter* noted below.

Printed sources

The quality newspapers tend to have weekly computing sections with news of new web services: *The Guardian* (Thursday), the *Telegraph* (Thursday), and *The Times* (Monday). Some of the contents are reproduced on the papers' websites (listed in Chapter 6). A selection of UK Internet magazines is listed in Chapter 13, and browsing through these can also be a useful way of keeping up-to-date with new sites. Again, they have websites which may include similar information. In addition, many general computer magazines such as *Computer Weekly* and *Personal Computer World* regularly provide updates on new resources and Internet developments.

General sources with a broad coverage

Many services try to cover all subjects and types of source, but can vary in how comprehensive and timely they actually are. Most are international in coverage, but some are limited or biased geographically.

The Heriot-Watt *Internet Resources Newsletter*
http://www.hw.ac.uk/libWWW/irn/irn.html
is a particularly useful source as it is produced monthly for the academic community in the UK by library staff at Heriot-Watt University. Subject-oriented resources are organized in sections by access method, with live links to the resources. However, there is a bias towards resources in science and technology, and business.

What's New (UK Yell)
http://www.yell.co.uk/ukyw/whats_new/index.html
lists all the sites added to the UK Yell web directory in recent weeks. You can limit by date and search by letter or by category.

What's new on Yahoo!
http://www.yahoo.com/new/
is the most comprehensive guide: it consists of the sources that have been added to the *Yahoo!* subject collection. Hundreds of items are usually listed each day.

What's new on Yahoo! UK & Ireland
http://www.yahoo.co.uk/new/
contains new UK resources.

Yahoo! Picks of the Week (sent by e-mail)
http://www.yahoo.com/picks/

UK Index's What's New This Week?
http://www.ukindex.co.uk/whatsnew.html
provides a weekly listing of new sites added to *UK Index*.

Net-happenings is a busy, moderated, announcements-only distribution list, which gathers announcements from many Internet sources and concentrates them into one list. There is a bias towards sites of educational value. *Net-happenings* is available as a discussion/distribution list; subscription information can be found at:

http://listserve.classroopm.com/archives/,
a newsgroup (**comp.internet.net-happenings**), and is archived on a
web server:
   http://listserve.classroom.com/archives/net-happenings.html

The **comp.infosystems.www.announce** newsgroup, with a large
number of postings per day, announces a range of new websites
(academic, commercial, recreational). If you don't have local access
to Usenet then try a public Usenet site such as *Deja.com* (see
Chapter 3).

Selective sources for education

The *BUBL LINK update*
   http://www.bubl.ac.uk/link/updates/current.html
is produced every two weeks, listing additions and changes to
BUBL's catalogue of Internet resources.

Each subject collection within *Infomine* Scholarly Internet Resource
Collections at
   http://infomine.ucr.edu/
has a 'What's New' feature, or the Alert Service can e-mail you
updates and additions:
   http://infomine.ucr.edu/email/

The *Scout Report* is a weekly publication offering a selection of
newly discovered Internet resources of interest to researchers and
educators. A brief description of each new resource is given. It is
accessed via the web with links to all listed resources, or by subscribing to an e-mail distribution list (full details from web page).
The UK mirror site is
   http://www.ilrt.bris.ac.uk/mirrors/scout/report/sr/current/
      index.html
Three subject-specific *Scout Reports* are also available: Business &
Economics, Science & Engineering, and Social Sciences.

Specialist sources

Discussion lists and electronic journals

There are specialist sources for new discussion lists and electronic journals. As distribution-list-based services they deliver announcements of new services by e-mail. Further information and subscription details for the following lists can be found from Diane Kovacs' *Directory of Scholarly and Professional E-Conferences* at
  http://www.n2h2.com/KOVACS/

★ **new-list** gives notification of new discussion lists worldwide
★ **new-lists** gives notification of new discussion lists for the UK higher education community
★ **newjour** gives notification of new electronic journals.

Search tools

Specialist sources also exist to keep you abreast of developments in the web search tools described in Chapter 9. If you are particularly interested in learning more about developments in this area, two resources to investigate are:

  Search Engine Watch
  http://searchenginewatch.com/

and

  Search Engine Showdown
  http://www.notess.com/search/
Both include features to alert you to the latest news on search engines.

Monitoring changes to Internet resources

Changes to Internet resources can be monitored with *Mind-it*
  http://minder.netmind.com/

This is a free but extremely effective service which enables you to register the URL of a web page you are interested in, and subsequently sends an e-mail message to inform you every time there is a change to this page. There is no limit to the number of URLs you can register with *Mind-it*. It is also possible to monitor part of a web page. Extensive user Help for *Mind-it* is available at:

http://minder.netmind.com/help.shtml

The Informant is a free service that can be used to track changes to specific web pages or specific search engine results. It will check these periodically, and send you e-mail whenever there are new or updated web pages:

http://informant.dartmouth.edu/

New and updated Internet software

In addition to sources listed in Chapter 6, *Catch-UP*

http://www.manageable.com/

is a free, web-based service that automatically searches for the newest versions of many popular Internet software applications. Configure the *Catch-UP* helper application and, with a simple click of a button, *Catch-UP* will generate a customized list of possible updates including corresponding download sites.

Covercd.co.uk

http://covercd.co.uk/

is a UK site which provides reviews and explanations of the software provided by the free cover CDs of the most widely available computer magazines.

Software agents

Intelligent agents are a software solution to keeping up-to-date with new resources. These programs gather information or perform some other service without your immediate presence and on some regular schedule. You provide the agents with information about your interests, and then they use that information to make informed suggestions for other Internet resources that may also be of interest. Another term for these agents is a 'bot' (short for robot), and the practice or technology of having information brought to you by an agent is sometimes referred to as push technology.

Agents have been developed that personalize information on a website based on registration information and usage analysis, while other types of agents include specific site watchers that tell you when the site has been updated or look for other events. There are analyst agents that not only gather but organize and interpret information for you. Some of these products are available free-of-charge, but commercial services are frequently charged.

A growing number of subject directories and portals offer the opportunity to customize your retrieval from their sites. In some cases this is through channels or a personalized service like *My Yahoo* at:

http://my.yahoo.com/

or *My Excite* at:

http://my.excite.com/

In addition, some online publications can also be personalized to your own interests.

An authoritative source of further information on intelligent agents is *BotSpot* at:

http://botspot.com/

11

Creating your own web page

Why publish?

These days any Internet user is able to be a publisher and have a potential readership of millions. Whether everyone *should* is, of course, another matter. Is there any benefit in putting up a personal home page with details of your interests and links to your favourite websites if it includes little of real value? Creating web pages about a particular band or actor will have wider appeal, but isn't necessarily a good use of your institution's computer system! Universities and colleges will usually permit personal pages, but they may limit the space that can be used and may close down services that are deemed inappropriate or create too much traffic on the local network – thus the Coronation Street site at Sheffield University had to move when it became too popular.

However, there are useful 'approved' applications, some of which may only be for local use rather than intended for the whole world. You could:

★ create a site as part of some coursework
★ provide information on behalf of a student society or your students' union

★ make your CV available
★ show images of work you have created, say in fine art or industrial design
★ detail the work of your research group
★ make available software you have written
★ publish substantial original information you have gathered on a
topic
★ make available a database you have created.

You need to consider whether what you want to publish is original,
interesting, accurate, up-to-date and in other ways of value. There
are a billion web pages out there, with many of doubtful value – be
sure yours is a worthwhile addition!

Remember that, as with e-mail, there are restrictions on what
you may publish. Offensive, obscene, racist and libellous material is
not allowed, and web pages on academic systems should not be
used for advertising or commercial purposes, nor should they
include copyright material unless you have specific permission to
do so. When requesting access to your local computer system you
will have agreed to abide by local conditions of use, and once you
are using JANET there is also the *JANET Acceptable Use Policy*
  http://www.ja.net/documents/use.html
These conditions are enforced. The general laws of a country apply
too. Remember that you are publishing internationally, so what may
be acceptable in one country may not be in another, for example,
blasphemy.

How to publish

Though you could have files that are accessible to users by FTP, most
people will make information available on the Internet by creating
web pages. How these are made available will vary between institutions depending on what sort of machine is used to host the pages
(the web server), so you will need to enquire, or you may find details
on your local web information service. On the other hand the

procedures for creating pages are based on using the Hypertext Markup Language (HTML) and so are the same everywhere.

Hypertext Markup Language (HTML)

There is not space here to do more than give a flavour of what HTML does, though the notes given will be sufficient to allow you to create very simple pages. There are also pointers to further information. As is noted later, there is software available to help you create pages but, nevertheless, some knowledge of the underlying principles helps you understand what is going on.

HTML is based on the principle of using tags, or markers, to indicate the formatting and structure of text, choice of colours, placing of images, and so on. This approach gives access to the information whatever the browser used, unlike a word-processed file or spreadsheet, which is accessible only to users with compatible software.

The layout that others will see is totally dependent on the tags and how the browser interprets them, not on how you lay out the page when you create it. Thus, text will flow continuously until told otherwise, and heading styles start where indicated and continue until the corresponding end-of-heading tag is reached. Different browsers will display the text in different ways, for example, where line breaks occur or in the amount of space above or below headings. Your browser will normally allow you to see the HTML file for any page you are viewing – for example, in Netscape choose 'View/Document Source' and in Internet Explorer choose 'View/Source'. This is helpful in learning how HTML works.

HTML and browsers are developing all the time, and there will be new HTML features supported in only the latest versions of browsers. You may not be able to use the latest version and even if you can you should remember that many of your users will not be able to see your pages as you intended if you use features not generally supported, so don't be too adventurous. You can see the official specification for HTML at

http://www.w3.org/MarkUp/

Basic HTML tags

Tags are normally used in matched pairs, one to indicate the beginning of a particular feature and the other the end. So a main heading is defined by <H1> and </H1> – note the / in the end tag.

The major tags are

<TITLE>	</TITLE>	A title to the whole document
<H1> to <H6>	</H1> etc	Headings of various size – H1 is the largest
<P>	no end tag	New paragraph – add a line space and start a new line
 	no end tag	Line break – start a new line
<HR>	no end tag	A horizontal line (or rule)
<UL>	</UL>	An unordered (bulleted) list
<OL>	</OL>	An ordered (numbered) list
<LI>	no end tag	Item in a list
<PRE>	</PRE>	Preformatted text – preserves the layout, including spaces and tabs. Other tags cannot be used in such text. This provides a simple way of laying out tables, for example.

Tags can be in upper or lower case, but the convention is to use upper case.

To link to other resources you create a hyperlink in the form:

<A HREF ="URL">*some text*</A> where *some text* is the highlighted link.

For example, if your document includes <A HREF="http://wxweb.msu.edu/weather">weather maps</A> then when the user clicks on the highlighted link text 'weather maps' the browser will display the page specified by the URL. If you are referring to a document on the same system as your pages you need give only the filename and not the complete URL.

Other features

Text can also be in a variety of fonts (typefaces and sizes), styles (italic, bold) and colours, though browsers can usually only interpret a few fonts correctly. You can have a coloured background to a page or include a pattern instead.

You may want to include images, such as photographs, a logo, graphs, charts, etc as illustrations or as buttons to act as hypertext links to other pages. These may be scanned from a print image, created in a paint program, be the output from other software such as a spreadsheet, or copied from clipart collections. Be aware that copyright applies so you shouldn't use other peoples' images without permission. (Images are often known as 'gifs', because the computer format frequently used is **.gif**, just as a word processed file is usually **.doc**.)

You can create tables either to present information in tabular form, or to design your page, since a table is an easy way to put text into columns. Each table comprises rectangles or 'cells' – the number depending on how many rows or columns you define in your table. Cells can have different types of content, background colours, font size, etc so can give a flexible layout. Tables are commonly used in home pages that need to point to many other pages on the site, such as on a portal site like *Yahoo! UK & Ireland* (**http://uk.yahoo.com/**).

Advanced techniques

The techniques mentioned above are straightforward for most people. Other techniques need much greater skills. These include using frames, where an outer part of the screen – typically a column at the left – contains contents information and remains static when other pages appear in the rest of the screen; and adding multimedia sources like animated images, video and sound. If you have a large site then you might want to have the facility to search for information within the pages. The latter needs more computing knowledge as does the use of Javascript which can, for example, automatically change a formatted date on a web page, cause a linked-to page to appear in a popup window or cause text or a graphic image to change when the mouse is placed on it (a 'rollover'). Java is a full programming language which can produce functions such as animations, calculators, and other fancy tricks.

Example

Figure 11.1 is a short piece of text in HTML, with Figure 11.2 showing how it would look with a graphical browser. It includes tags for tables and typefaces.

```
<P><CENTER><TABLE WIDTH="95%" BORDER="1" CELLSPACING="2" CELLPADDING="0">
<TR>
 <TD WIDTH="100%">
  <H3><CENTER> <FONT SIZE="+3" FACE="Britannic Bold">
  Key skills  - some useful resources</FONT></CENTER></H3>
 </TD>
 </TR>

</TABLE></CENTER></P>
<P<FONT SIZE="-1" FACE="Verdana">This page has a selection of resources relating to study and IT skills,
particularly for distance learners. Suggestions for additions are welcome.</FONT></P>

<H3><CENTER><FONT FACE="Comic Sans MS">General - background and material on all topics
</FONT></CENTER></H3>

<P>
<FONT SIZE="-1" FACE="Verdana"><BR>
<A HREF="http://www.coun.uvic.ca/learn/hndouts.html">Learning  skills handouts</A> </FONT>
<FONT SIZE="-2" FACE="Verdana">(University of Victoria, Canada)<BR>
</FONT><FONT SIZE="-1" FACE="Verdana">
<A HREF="http://www.muskingum.edu /~cal/database/genpurpose.html">Learning strategies </A></FONT>
<FONT SIZE="-2" FACE="Verdana">(Muskingum College)<BR>
```

Fig. 11.1   *A sample HTML file*

Key skills - some useful resources

This page has a selection of resources relating to study and IT skills, particularly for distance learners. Suggestions for additions are welcome.

General - background and material on all topics

Learning skills handouts (University of Victoria, Canada)
Learning strategies (Muskingum College)

Fig. 11.2   *The result of an HTML file in a web browser*

Learning to create pages

You may actually be taught to write pages as part of your course, otherwise you can find out from books, but there are so many manuals available, with new ones appearing frequently, that mentioning any particular ones is pointless. There are, of course, guides on the web itself.

Useful basic guides to HTML include:

Beginners Guide to HTML
**http://www.ncsa.uiuc.edu/General/Internet/WWW/
HTMLPrimer.html**

How Do They Do That in HTML?
http://www.nashville.net/~carl/htmlguide/

and others can be found from collections such as

HTML Goodies
http://htmlgoodies.earthweb.com/

NetLearn: Web Based Learning Resources
http://www.rgu.ac.uk/~sim/research/netlearn/html.htm

The Netskills organization at Newcastle University runs courses for UK higher education about the Internet, including web publishing. Unless you are a research student you probably won't be able to attend a course, but your library or computing service may use some of their training material, or if your institution has a licence you can download it yourself from

http://www.netskills.ac.uk/materials/

Other sites can help you with graphics resources and advanced techniques:

Web Design Resources
http://www.windweaver.com/searchpage7.htm

Web Developer's Virtual Library
http://WWW.Stars.com/

Web Places
http://www.webplaces.com/search/

Web Publishing: Supporting Links
http://www.sbu.ac.uk/lis/training/html/links.html

Webmonkey
http://www.hotwired.com/webmonkey/

There are also *Usenet* groups and discussion lists that you can use to keep up with developments and to get help from other users. These include: **comp.infosystems.www.authoring.html**, **comp.infosystems.www.authoring.images** and the list **html-1** at **vm.ege.edu.tr**

Web publishing software

Though HTML documents can be created by text editors such as *Windows Notepad* or *Emacs* on Unix, for most people this is extremely tedious for anything other than simple pages with few links. Fortunately there are editing programs you can use such as *Dreamweaver*, *FrontPage*, *HotDog*, *HoTMetaL*, *HTML Assistant*, *Netscape Composer* and *PageMill*. These can be similar in principle to word-processing packages – indeed Word can be used to create pages – in that they allow you to create the page the way you want it to look; the program then translates it into HTML code for you. Creating tables, specifying colours, adding images etc can be straightforward, though these packages don't always do exactly what you want, so you may still have to amend the HTML code.

You will need to check with your computing service to see what is available to you, or you can find a free package like *webWeaver* from a software archive like *UK Mirror Service* (Chapter 6).

Designing effective pages

You don't have to be a graphic designer to put together web pages, but you do have to think about what will make them effective. A general principle might be that the content and its organization is more important than the visual appearance of the pages. Among useful guidelines are:

★ Make clear on the first page what the intention of your website is and what it contains.

★ If you want a maximum audience for your pages, then they should be predominantly plain text and not have technically advanced features like Java or Flash multimedia. In general don't let effects obscure the content. If you need these features tell users what browser and plug-ins are needed and consider whether you need to offer a text version as an alternative. Preferably don't require a particular screen size.

★ Images and other multimedia content may make a page look more interesting, but can take a long time to download – particularly if users are using a dialup connection – and they might give up waiting, so don't include them unnecessarily. With still images consider using small ones such as icons as decoration or 'thumbnail' pictures, that can link to larger images if users wish to. You can also use techniques that can compress them to a smaller file size. Don't have too many on any page.

★ Give some alternative text to images, especially if the image is the hyperlink. Users of graphical browsers may have the images turned off for speed.

★ Backgrounds (plain or fancy) that obscure text, and text that blinks or floats around the screen may well annoy users.

★ Don't have a document more than a few screens long unless you have a contents list at the top with links to 'anchors' in the appropriate parts of the text. Long documents are difficult to browse through.

★ If you have a large number of pages give thought to the 'navigation' – how users will find their way around. They should always know where they are, with links back to important pages like your home page. It should be clear what information a link is taking them to.

★ Test your hyperlinks to ensure they work when you have written the page, but also regularly to ensure they stay correct. You can use a link checking service to do this, for example *Net Mechanic* (**http://www.netmechanic.com/**).

★ If you can, test your pages with different browsers and different versions, to see that they display as you intend. For example, some versions of graphical browsers cannot deal well with colours or particular fonts. A service called *Bobby* (**http://www.cast.org/bobby/**) can do this testing and also checks for accessibility by the disabled. *WebSiteGarage* (**http://WebSiteGarage.com/**) provides a number of tests, including estimating how long your page will take to download at different modem speeds.

★ Make your pages consistent in style.

★ Include a date, your name and e-mail address.

★ Link to your institution's home pages.

You can, of course, find guidance online:

Accessible Web Design
http://www.adesignabove.com/business/articles/intro.html

Alertbox: Current Issues in Web Usability
http://www.useit.com/alertbox
is a bimonthly column focusing each time on a particular aspect of usability.

Guide to Good Practices for WWW Authors
http://www.man.ac.uk/MVC/SIMA/Isaacs/title.html

Usability Issues in Web Site Design
http://info.lboro.ac.uk/research/husat/inuse/f3_web_paper.html

The Web Developer's Virtual Library: Style Guidelines
http://WWW.Stars.com/Seminars/Style/

Web Style Manual
http://info.med.yale.edu/caim/manual/

Announcing your pages

Once created, your pages will be available to anyone using your university/college system and, provided access is not restricted to your campus only, eventually to users of search services. However, you may want to announce them to the wider world.

If your pages have a particular subject content you could send a message to an appropriate discussion list or newsgroup giving the URL and a brief description of the content. If there is a subject collection covering your topic you may wish to contact that too. You can also submit details to the general 'what's new' services discussed in the previous chapter and to web search services, which often have an 'Add URL' or 'Submit Site' option. For some guidance on how to publicize pages see

Promoting your pages
http://osu.orst.edu/aw/promote/

Alternatively you can use services such as

Selfpromotion.com
http://selfpromotion.com/

or

Submit It!
http://www.submit-it.com/

12

Citing electronic sources in your work

★ Recommendations for citing

When you complete an essay, dissertation or other piece of written work, you are usually expected to refer to (or 'cite') the publications you have used. This is to make it clear to anyone reading (and marking) the piece where your information has come from. These references need to be precise, giving the publication, date, pages, article title, etc, and there are standard ways of setting out references that you may be expected to use. So as you make more use of electronic sources, such as CD-ROMs and the Internet, you need to refer to them in a similar way as to printed sources. Procedures for citing electronic sources are not yet as established as for printed sources, but there are some commonly used conventions.

As with citing printed sources, the important principle is to be consistent in the way you refer to the same sort of publication, and to include all the relevant detail needed to enable someone to find the source. Given the way the Internet changes it is also important to note the date you used a resource, since the content may have changed since then.

Generally recommended formats for citing Internet sources are:

World wide web

Title (underline or italics)

URL
Date accessed (square brackets)
Example: <u>Student grants and loans: a brief guide for higher education students.</u>
URL: http://www.open.gov.uk/dfee/loans/loans.htm [12 September 1999]

E-mail correspondence

Author
Date (in round brackets)
Subject (underline or italics)
'e-mail to' recipient's name (in square brackets)
[online]
'Available e-mail:' recipient's e-mail address
Example: Corliss, B (16 September 1997) <u>News from Seattle</u> [e-mail to T. Wright] [online] Available e-mail: twright@uvmvm.uvm.edu

Journal article from e-mail

Author
Title (not underlined or italicized)
Journal title (underlined or italics)
Type of medium (square brackets)
Volume (issue), date and paging (if given)
'Available e-mail:' e-mail address
Example: Sloan, B Crime statistics: how valid? <u>Social work review</u> [online] 2(3) March 1995. Available e-mail: swr@howard.gov.uk

Discussion list message

Author
Date (round brackets)
Subject

Discussion-list name (underline or italics)
[online]
'Available e-mail:' e-mail address
Example: Roseman, M (7 June 1996) WWW guide for historians
<u>German-history discussion list</u> [online] Available e-mail: german-history@mailbase.ac.uk

Complete discussion list

List name (underline or italic)
[online]
'Available e-mail:' e-mail address
Example: <u>Algeria news list</u> [online] Available e-mail: ALGE-NEWS@gwuvm.gwu.edu

Usenet messages

Author
Date (round brackets)
Subject (underline or italics)
[discussion]
[online]
'Available Usenet newsgroup:' name of the group
Example: Tranholm, S (8 January 1993) <u>2001: a space odyssey</u> [discussion] [online] Available Usenet newsgroup: alt.cult-movies

FTP

Author
Date (included with the source – round brackets)
Title (underline or italics)
[online]
'Available FTP:' address; directory; file; date accessed (square brackets)
Example: King, ML (August 1963) <u>I have a dream</u> [online]

Available FTP: mrcnext.cso.uiuc.edu; directory: gutenberg/freenet; file: i-have-a-dream; [2 March 1998]

Telnet

Author
Date (round brackets – put 'no date' if there is no date in the source)
Title (underline or italics)
[online]
'Available telnet:' address; directory: file; date accessed (square brackets)
Example: Perot, R (1992) <u>An America in danger</u> [online] Available telnet: gopher.tc.umn.edu; directory: libraries/electronic books; file: An America in Danger; [14 June 1999]

If you need further guidance ask your library staff or see if the library has the following books:

Lester, J. D., *Citing cyberspace*, Addison Wesley Longman, 1997.
Li, X. & Crane, N., *Electronic Styles: An Expanded Guide to Citing Electronic Information,* 2nd edn, Information Today, 1996.

Excerpts from the latter can be found at
  http://www.uvm.edu/~ncrane/estyles.html

There is a *Guide to Citing Internet Sources* at
  http://www.bournemouth.ac.uk/using_the_library/html/
  guide_to_citing_internet_sourc.html

and

  Cite them right!
  http://www.unn.ac.uk/central/isd/cite/
is a guide to citing all kinds of publications, including Internet sources.

13

What next?

★ Local support
★ Online guides
★ Collections of Internet guides and training
   resources
★ Books and magazines

Local support

This book can only discuss the Internet in general terms. Staff at
your institution can provide specific information on which services
are available to you and how to use them. Either the library or the
computing centre is likely to provide local documentation (increasingly published on the local web pages), and they may run demonstrations or courses about the Internet. In particular, they may offer
training material produced by *Netskills* (see below). Commercial
Internet training is expensive, so do take advantage of the assis-
tance and resources freely provided while you are a student!

The Netskills project
http://www.netskills.ac.uk/
was originally established to provide Internet training and training
resources for UK higher education. *Netskills* training materials are
now available for purchase, with educational discounts. Check
with your library or computing centre to see if your institution has
a site licence for access to some or all of the *Netskills* modules.

If you are not sure where to start, ask at the Help or Enquiry points in your library or computer centre.

Online guides

The Online Netskills Interactive Course (TONIC)
http://www.netskills.ac.uk/TONIC/
is a web-based learning course on using the Internet produced by *Netskills* (see above). *TONIC* is an easy-to-understand, structured course, offering step-by-step practical guidance on major Internet topics, progressing from basic through to advanced. The course as a whole is intended for beginners to networking who have some familiarity with computers. The course provides an introduction to the Internet and computer networks in general, describing and illustrating the main software tools for navigating the networks. It looks at types and examples of networked information, at the means for searching that information, and at the communication facilities and resources on the Net.

TONIC is designed to give the user practice with using various Internet services, and to provide feedback on progress. There are exercises, simulations, animations, optional self-assessment tests, and the opportunity to e-mail your comments. A system of registration makes it possible for you to follow through the course in a systematic way, and to go straight to the point where you left off in a previous session. Helpful links will orient you and enable you to take alternative paths through the material are provided throughout.

Some other online guides are listed below:

Internet Detective
http://sosig.ac.uk/desire/internet-detective.html
An interactive tutorial on evaluating the quality of Internet resources.

Sink or Swim: Internet Search Tools and Techniques
http://www.lboro.ac.uk/info/training/finding/sink.htm
A guide to effective searching on the Internet, with comparisons of major search engines.

Introducing the Internet (biz/ed)
http://www.bized.ac.uk/fme/internet.htm
Introduction to major Internet concepts, search engines, copyright and citations.

The UK Index Beginners Guide: the Net
http://www.ukindex.co.uk/begin0.html
Brief introduction to the WWW, e-mail, FTP, Internet tools, jargon, viruses and netiquette.

WebWise (BBC Education)
http://www.bbc.co.uk/webwise/
Over 1,000 pages of help, advice and news on how to get the best out of the Internet.

Internet Tutorials (University of Albany Libraries)
http://www.albany.edu/library/internet/
Over 20 beginners' tutorials to the Internet. Categories cover basic Internet, research guides, search engines, browsers, and software training.

Internet Web Text (John December)
http://www.december.com/web/text/index.html
Excellent guide to all aspects of the Internet; regularly updated.

net.TUTOR (Ohio State University)
http://gateway.lib.ohio-state.edu/tutor/
Provides interactive learning modules on concepts, tools and techniques for becoming an effective Internet researcher.

TOURBUS
http://www.TOURBUS.com/
A free, on-going, semi-weekly, text-based tour of some of the neatest sites on the Internet; the archives may also be browsed.

Collections of Internet guides and training resources

Internet Guides, Tutorials and Training Information
http://lcweb.loc.gov/global/internet/training.html
links to resources collected by the Library of Congress, which originate from a range of organizations.

NetLearn
http://www.rgu.ac.uk/~sim/research/netlearn/callist.htm
from the Robert Gordon University, is a directory of resources for learning and teaching Internet skills. Evaluative annotations are provided for resources covering: learning, teaching, navigating and providing information on the Internet; learning HTML; demographics; special needs and foreign language resources.

TERENA Guide to Network Resource Tools
http://www.terena.nl/libr/gnrt/
This reference source helps users discover how to carry out common networking tasks, how and where on the network to search for information, which tools are available, where to find them and how to use them.

Books

Publishing books about the Internet is certainly a growth industry. Your library will hold many relevant titles, and doing a keyword or subject search on 'Internet' or 'web' in the library catalogue should retrieve most of them. If you decide to buy a book about the Internet (in addition to this one!), do be cautious, as price is no indication of quality. Always ensure that you have purchased the most up-to-date edition – your library, and many bookshops, should have reference sources to enable you to check this.

You can also check details at the

Computer Manuals Online Bookstore
http://www.compman.co.uk/

or one of the increasing number of online bookstores. A list of bookshops is available from NISS:

http://www.niss.ac.uk/lis/bookshops.html

Do look at the contents of the book before purchase – if you mainly intend to access the Internet through JANET, you will not need to pay for pages discussing which Information Service Provider (ISP) to select, nor will you require an extensive knowledge of Unix unless you plan to run your own server. A book which merely lists the URLs of Internet resources (often called Internet *Yellow Pages*) will quickly date – it is much better to consult a library copy.

Reviews of Internet Books by a Canadian writer, Rob Slade, are available at:

http://victoria.tc.ca/int-grps/books/techrev/mnbk.htm

Online editions of computer and Internet books can be found in the

Online Electronic Publishing Collection: Computer & Internet Books:
http://hoganbooks.com/freebook/webbooks.html

and also at the

InformIT Free Library
http://www.informit.com/itlibrary/
Registration is required for this service:
http://www.informit.com/Login/

Popular magazines

There are a considerable number of UK Internet magazines. They will contain Internet news, product reviews, lists of new resources, answers to readers' queries, guides to sources on specific topics and so on, although the emphasis is mostly on the recreational uses of the Net. You might like to check to see if your library (or a local public library) subscribes, as they cost around £3–£4 an issue, and much of the information dates quickly. Their websites, listed below, will indicate the coverage and content of the magazines, and these sites are a useful source for news items in themselves, usually including some of the contents of each issue.

These magazines are also particularly useful for providing up-to-date information on pricing and options offered by commercial Internet Service Providers (ISPs).

.net (Future Publishing)
http://www.netmag.co.uk/

Internet Advisor (Future Publishing)
http://www.netadvisor.co.uk/

Internet Made Easy (Paragon Publishing)
http://binky.paragon.co.uk/internetme/index.html

Internet Magazine (EMAP)
http://www.internet-magazine.com/

Practical Internet (Paragon Publishing)
http://binky.paragon.co.uk/pi/index.html

Web Pages Made Easy (Paragon Publishing)
http://binky.paragon.co.uk/webpages/

What's Online (Paragon Publishing)
http://binky.paragon.co.uk/whats/index.html

US-based magazines with extensive websites include:

Internet World
http://www.internetworld.com/

Wired (Wired Ventures Ltd)
http://www.wired.com/wired/

Yahoo! Internet Life
http://www.zdnet.com/yil/

Reviews for those Internet magazines and journals that have been reviewed in the 'Internet in Print' section of the *Internet Resources Newsletter* are available at:

http://www.hw.ac.uk/libWWW/irn/inprint.html

Now it's up to you . . .

This book will have given you an outline of what the Internet is, and an indication of what it can be used for. We have included details of many information sources, and information on how to locate others. In this final chapter we have given further suggestions on how you may develop to a greater depth the skills and knowledge discussed throughout the book. If you have used the Internet before, then we hope you can use this book to learn of new sources and services useful for further and higher education. If you are a newcomer to the Net, then now is the time to take the plunge – if that is the right word – and start exploring. This book is a guide to help you to see what the Internet can do for you – your only limitations are your imagination and the time available to you!

14

Jargon explained

Acrobat Reader Software used with a **browser** to allow the display of documents using the **PDF** format.

AHDS (Arts and Humanities Data Service) Information services for UK higher education.

applet A small **Java** program that can be embedded in an **HTML** page, for example, to provide some animation.

Archie Utility that maintains a searchable database of the contents of **file archive** sites.

ASCII (American Standard Code for Information Interchange) Standard way of encoding characters, numbers and symbols. Plain text files are sometimes referred to as ASCII files.

ATHENS An **authentication** system used to give access to various information services for UK higher education such as the **BIDS** databases.

authentication A process, often using usernames and passwords, to verify that users have the right to a particular service, such as one to which a university subscribes.

bandwidth Strictly the difference (measured in Hz), between the highest and lowest frequencies of a transmission, but used loosely to refer to the transmission capacity of the lines that carry the **Internet**'s electronic traffic. The bandwidth will vary on different parts of the network, for example the transatlantic section has much less capacity than many local networks.

BIDS (Bath Information and Data Services) A range of services, especially bibliographic databases, for UK higher education.

binary Notation using only the digits 0 and 1 – the simplest form used by a computer. Files retrieved by **FTP** may often be in binary.

Boolean Boolean logic is the use of 'operators' (words) like AND, OR, NOT and NEAR to specify a combination of words to be searched for in a file or database

browser Software to view **world wide web** documents. Examples include Netscape Navigator and Microsoft Internet Explorer for graphical use, and *Lynx* for text only.

cache A temporary storage of web pages so that subsequent requests for the same pages do not have to go to the original location, so reducing long distance **network traffic**. A cache may be just on your machine; at your institution storing pages accessed by any users; or a national service.

CGI (Common Gateway Interface) CGI is a method used by web pages to communicate with programs run on the web server, for example, putting the content of a form into an e-mail message, or searching a database.

client A program that is used to contact and obtain data from a **server**, often across a great distance. A web **browser** is a client.

compression Procedures to pack files into a smaller size to reduce storage requirements and speed up transfer across networks. Filenames for compressed files have extensions such as .zip and .tar. Compressed files must be uncompressed before they can be used.

conferencing Using **discussion lists** and **newsgroups** to communicate, share information or debate particular subjects.

cookie A cookie is a short file put on your system by a **browser** which includes information about your usage and helps the current use. For example, it may include the information that you have already logged into a passworded area in the current session and don't need a second password check.

dataset Collection of numerical and bibliographic data made available for searching across the Internet. UK examples are *BIDS* and *MIDAS*.

discussion list E-mail-based subject **conference**.

DNS (Domain Name System) The DNS is a service housed on a number of servers across the Internet which maintains a database for converting between domain names and **IP addresses**. This allows users to specify remote computers by host names rather than numerical **IP addresses**.

domain name Unique alphabetic representation of a computer's location on the Internet. Compare **IP address**.

download To transfer a file, image, software or other material from a remote computer to your own.

EDINA Information services for UK higher education provided from Edinburgh University.

e-mail (electronic mail) System which enables messages to be sent from one person's computer (or space on a central computer) to another.

electronic journal (e-journal) A journal/periodical published across the Internet. It may exist only in electronic format or may be an electronic version of a printed publication.

FAQ (Frequently Asked Questions) Common questions and answers about a particular topic are often collected in a FAQ file, which is updated as necessary and reissued periodically, commonly on a **newsgroup**.

file archive Collection of files – such as software, numerical data, texts – that can be retrieved by **FTP**.

frames A way of designing web pages that has an outer column or row on the page that remains permanent while text on the rest of the page can change. Commonly used for a list of contents to a site.

FTP (File Transfer Protocol) A standard **protocol** (and an application) which permits files to be copied from one computer to another, regardless of file format or operating system.

GIF (Graphic Interchange Format) A common format for image files, especially suitable for images containing large areas of the same colour, for example, a logo, and for line drawings. GIF format files can be used for photographs but **JPEG** is preferred.

helper Software used in association with a **browser** to display particular types of file, such as a Microsoft Word document. Similar to a **plug-in**.

host A computer system which provides a service, such as **e-mail** or access to a database.

HTML (Hypertext Markup Language) The coding system used for creating documents on the **world wide web** that can be read using a **browser**.

HTTP (Hypertext Transfer Protocol) The search and retrieval **protocol** used for transferring **HTML** documents.

hypertext Text that contains links to other text, allowing information to be retrieved nonsequentially.

hypermedia Electronic media – text, graphics, video, sound – linked to provide information.

ingenta A company providing information services such as the *BIDS* databases and **electronic journals**.

interface Strictly the user interface – the way in which a user communicates with a program. In the Internet context we are normally referring to a graphical user interface (GUI) like Windows or a **browser**. Good interface design is important to make using a website or service a simple process.

Internet The worldwide collection of interconnected computer networks.

Internet Service Provider (ISP) A company providing (sometimes free) access to the Internet for anyone.

Intranet A private network inside an organization that uses the same kinds of software, such as a web **browser**, **HTML** files, that you would find on the public **Internet**, but that is usually only for internal use. So some teaching or administrative material on university web systems may be restricted to that university only.

IP address Unique numeric representation of a computer's location on the Internet. It comprises four sets of numbers separated by periods. Compare **domain name.**

JANET (Joint Academic Network) The computer network linking UK higher and further education institutions and research organizations.

Java A programming language that can be used to create applications such as animation and multimedia for web pages.

Javascript A script language (with little in common with **Java**) developed by Netscape for writing short programs embedded in a web page.

JPEG (Joint Photographic Experts Group) JPEG is a common format for image files and is best for full-colour or grey-scale photographic-type, digital images.

Listserv A common **utility** used to manage **discussion lists** on the Internet.

Lynx A text-only web **browser**.

Mailbase The organization which manages and promotes the use of **discussion lists** for UK higher education.

metasearch A metasearch service allows the searching of a number of web search services from one search screen.

MIMAS (Manchester InforMation and Associated Services) A service for UK higher education providing economic and social statistics, bibliographic databases and electronic journals.

MIME (Multipurposes Internet Mail Extensions) The standard for attaching non-text files to standard Internet mail messages. Non-text files include graphics, spreadsheets, formatted word-processor documents, sound files, etc. It is also used by web **servers** to identify the files – such as sound, video, etc, they are sending to browsers.

mirror A mirror site is an exact copy of a web or **FTP** site in another geographical location so as to improve local access. Popular sites may have mirrors in various parts of the world.

MPEG (Moving Pictures Experts Group) A format that defines the standard of performance in audio and video playback.

Netscape The company producing Netscape Navigator, the most common graphical **browser** for the **world wide web**. The browser itself is usually referred to just as Netscape.

network traffic The flow of information in local, national and international networks. Excessive network traffic leads to slower responses to information requests.

newsgroups The hierarchically arranged collection of topic areas in **Usenet**.

newsreader Software needed to read **newsgroups**. It may be included in a web **browser**.

NISS (National Information Services and Systems) The organization providing the *NISS* information service for UK education.

OPAC (Online Public Access Catalogue) A contrived name for a computerized library catalogue.

PDF (Portable Document Format) The format used by Adobe Acrobat software for representing documents containing text, graphics, and images in a manner that is independent of the original application software, hardware, and operating system used to create those documents. A PDF version of a printed document will look virtually identical to the original..

plug-in A (usually small) piece of optional software that adds features to a larger program. Web **browsers** like Netscape Navigator use plug-ins for multimedia files, compressed text, sound, etc. As browsers develop such features will become standard.

port A connection to a computer system, through which data can be exchanged.

portal A web page that provides access to many other services, maybe in a particular subject. Academic gateways like *BUBL* and the home pages of **Internet Service Providers** like Freeserve can be seen as portals.

protocol A well-defined set of data-exchange rules that apply to communication between computer systems.

search engine Software that searches a database. Commonly used to describe services that search the content of the **world wide web.**

server A computer which provides software and services across a local, national or international network.

spam The **Internet** version of junk mail. Spamming is sending the same message to a large number of people, mailing lists or **newsgroups**, usually to advertise something. It is not a practice that is encouraged.

SuperJANET The upgraded version of **JANET** that has greater speed and capacity, particularly for transmitting still and moving images and sound.

Swetsnet Sservice providing access to **electronic journals.**

telnet A standard **protocol** (and an application) that permits a user to log onto a remote computer system.

tool Another word for **utility.**

Unix A computer operating system that is commonly used on machines offering **Internet** services.

URL (Uniform Resource Locator) Standard naming/addressing system for files on the **Internet.**

Usenet Worldwide **conferencing** system comprising thousands of **newsgroups** on a huge range of subjects.

utility A program for a particular small task, such as managing **e-mail** or creating **HTML** text.

virus A small program that is designed to create mischief or damage on computers. Viruses can be downloaded with other software, found on the disks on the covers of magazines, or obtained in other unintended ways. Your computer should have an antivirus program to detect viruses.

VRML (Virtual Reality Modelling Language) The programming language used to create virtual reality applications across the Internet.

VT100 A standard for terminal display that is usually needed for **telnet** connections.

WAP (Wireless Application Protocol) A telecommunications technique that connects mobile phones to the **Internet.**

WWW (world wide web) The part of the **Internet** consisting of **hypermedia**, and needing a **browser** to view its pages.

For extensive glossaries of terms see:

Glossary of Internet Terms
http://www.delphi.com/navnet/glossary/

ILC Glossary of Internet Terms
http://www.matisse.net/files/glossary.html

Netlingo
http://www.netlingo.com/

Index

This is an index to concepts and applications. Specific Internet resources are excluded, apart from a few with wide usage.

———